Hoods
by the Armful

Academic Dress
AND THE Founding OF THE
Burgon Society

Philip Goff

The Burgon Society
London

TRANSACTIONS OF THE BURGON SOCIETY

Hoods by the Armful
Academic Dress and the Founding of the Burgon Society

A Special Issue of *Transactions of the Burgon Society*, 20 (2020).

First published by the Burgon Society, London, 2021.
Printed by Henry Ling Ltd, The Dorset Press, Dorchester, Dorset.
ISBN 978-1-8380679-2-2
Copyright © Philip Francis Michael Goff 2021

This work is set in Miller type.

Front cover photo Fellows and guests enjoy a guided tour of Charterhouse by the Master (who was then the Vice-Patron of the Society), Dr James Thomson, following the 2001 Congregation in London.

Hoods
by the Armful

Contents

Introduction

On the Facebook Academical Dress group site, upon learning that the Burgon Society was nearly twenty-one years old, a Cambridge academic (Dr John F Mueller Director of Studies in History, St Edmund's College, University of Cambridge) remarked: 'I'm shocked. Surely old men interested in pretty academic frocks is not an invention of this century.'[1] He was absolutely right, of course, and those of us who were the founders of the Burgon Society (some of whom, justifiably, may be described as 'old men' now but who were considerably younger then) were well aware that we were simply the latest devotees in a long line of admirers that perhaps stretched back to the twelfth century.[2]

What made us different, however, was the invention of the World Wide Web which enabled us to find and contact one another and thereby create a web of our own to further our study and enjoyment of this admittedly niche area of costume and to share, and record, information online.

The twentieth anniversary seemed an appropriate time to set out a record of how the Burgon Society was formed and by whom. The passing years, pleasingly, have brought a new generation of officers, fellows and members. However, those of us who were there at the beginning continue to meet and talk amongst ourselves and there has been a growing sense that it would be timely for us to tell

---

1 As Professor Bruce Christianson pointed out, the Burgon Society was founded at the end of the last century but the quip is too good to waste!

2 The Society is a child of the internet, although the interest goes back many years. T. W. Wood, *Ecclesiastical and Academical Colours* (London and Derby: Bemrose & Sons, [1875]), Frank W. Haycraft, *The Degrees and Hoods of the World's Universities and Colleges*, 1st edn (Ware, Herts.: privately printed by Jennings & Bewley, 1923). 'And from 1858 almost 20 years of discussion about hoods and gowns in Notes and Queries', Dr Nicholas Groves.

our story. The catalyst for writing this account came from the present-day officers of the Society via an email from the Editor of Transactions of the Burgon Society, Professor Stephen Wolgast who, writing about the forthcoming twentieth anniversary celebrations of the Society, said:

> More to the point of the anniversary, the executive committee suggested highlighting articles from our founders in the 20th go-round of TBS [Transactions of the Burgon Society], and ... I may be asking if you would consider contributing a short, first-person account of ye olden days, or of some aspect of the Society you would like to see saved for posterity in ink & pixel. How does all that sound?

This was seconded by one of the other founders, Professor Bruce Christianson, who is also on the editorial team of Transactions and was Dean of Studies for over thirteen years. It therefore seemed a good idea to set out to gather the memories of the founders whilst we are all still alive, although a 'short' account would not have done justice to the story.[3]

---

3 Since writing this, the sad news of the death of Dr Robin Rees FBS, one of the founding Fellows, has been announced.

1
Is There Anybody Out There?

In just a few decades, followers of the arcane area of costume known as academical dress had spread from a small number of independent scholars, authors and devotees, relying on the few published works, encyclopaedia entries, visits to libraries and university ceremonies, into a network of people sharing typewritten and duplicated notes, and writing letters to robemakers and universities; then early internet chatgroups, the Burgon Society, founded in 2000 to promote and study the subject, and now the Academic Dress Facebook Group and Twitter account.

So, what had sparked our interest? Some of us were at schools at which teachers wore academic gowns on a daily basis, with hoods on various special occasions. Others became interested whilst at university and others whilst attending church services or singing in a church choir.

Many of us, as children, had discovered, in our local libraries, the listings in *Pears' Cyclopaedia* of 'University Degrees Colours of Hoods' and eagerly awaited every new edition with its news of the dress of additional universities.[1] Although I didn't see or own a copy until the 1970s, a scholarly account of academic costume in Europe was published in 1963 and was the cause of many visits to the reference section of various libraries, in order to read it, in a time before photocopiers were widely available or the phone cameras were invented.[2]

1 'Academical Hoods' in the General Compendium. (Think Google and Wikipedia in a single volume). Between 1953 and 2017, *Pears'* was a national institution.

2 W. N. Hargreaves-Mawdsley, *A History Of Academical Dress In Europe Until The End Of The Eighteenth Century* (Oxford: Clarendon Press, 1963).

Of enormous importance to many of us fascinated by this subject, in our generation, was the publication in 1966, of Dr George Shaw's *Academical Dress of British Universities*.[3] The book made many aware of the subject and inspired others to take it up as a hobby.[4] Dr Shaw had long been interested in the subject and pursued it whilst he was biology master at Lancing College, in Sussex. In 1970, Professor Hugh Smith's enormous 3-volume work on academic dress was published,[5] as was Charles Franklyn's inscrutable and seemingly haphazard volume.[6] And in 1972, The Degrees and Hoods of the World's Universities and Colleges,[7] an unauthorised update of Frank Haycraft's earlier work went to press.[8] All of these books looked back to earlier works by the Revd Thomas Wood and the various earlier editions of Haycraft, although in his lesser-known volume, Dr Thomas Baty claimed not to have known about the work but is complimentary about Wood.[9] No doubt Wood, in his time, had also known of other sources, perhaps now lost to us.

In early 1974, an occasional typed newsletter concerning academic hoods, copied onto foolscap sheets, was begun and edited by Squadron Leader Alan Birt,[10] assisted later by Dr Robin Rees.[11] It was circulated to a subscription list for the cost of the stamps.

Academical Dress of British and Irish Universities, Dr Shaw's second edition of his 1966 book, was published in 1995.[12] The book contains many inaccuracies but nevertheless is an important contri-

---

3   George Wenham shaw, MA, DPhil, DSc, F.I. Biol. (1928–2006). His book was published by W. Heffer & Sons Ltd, Cambridge.

4   I clearly remember receiving a copy of it on my fourteenth birthday, from my parents, and colleagues tell similar stories.

5   Hugh Smith and Kevin Sheard, *Academic Dress and Insignia of the World* (A.A. Balkema, Capetown, 1970).

6   Charles A. H. Franklyn, *Academical Dress from the Middle Ages to the Present Day, Including Lambeth Degrees* (Lewes: printed privately by W. E. Baxter, Ltd., 1970).

7   Frank W. Haycraft, 5th edn, rev. and enlarged by Frederick R. S. Rogers, Franklyn, Shaw, Hugh Alexander Boyd (Lewes: privately printed by W. E. Baxter, Ltd., 1972.

8   4th edn, rev. (Cheshent: privately printed by Cheshunt Press, 1948).

9   *Academic Colours* (Tokyo: Kenkyusha Press, 1934).

10   Squadron Leader Alan Edward Birt, BSc, ACP, FBS.

11   Robin Rees, MSc, MPhil, PhD, FBS.

12   Published by Phillimore in Chichester, West Sussex

bution to the published works on the subject containing, as it does, listings for several new universities.[13]

The people

Several of the Burgon Society's founders, amongst others we hadn't yet discovered, knew and, perhaps, owned at least some of these works and from the mid-twentieth century we were engaged, mostly independently, in collecting such information as was available at the time, along with collections of gowns and hoods and visits to libraries and robemaking companies. Perhaps, therefore, before we arrive at the birth of the Burgon Society some information about who we were is worth recording.

Philip Goff: Funny bits of silk and fur

In my own case, as I have written about before,[14] my interest in gowns and hoods began around the age of ten when I was a chorister in my parish church choir. Sitting behind the officiants and preachers at Matins and Evensong, I became aware of what a former Dean of St Paul's called 'those funny bits of silk and fur'.[15] The hoods sparked an earlier memory and I found a colour plate of some of them in one of the volumes of a set of encyclopaedias at home called *The Book of Knowledge*, edited by Gordon Stowell.[16] A year or so later I was at secondary school and began to see gowns more often, occasionally with their hoods. My interest was further awakened and many conversations with the clergy and my teachers followed (much to their amusement), although one of my teachers was something of a hood collector and had a string of degrees and diplomas.

Around this time, I bought an Ottoman silk Oxford MA hood[17] from Ede & Ravenscroft by sending in weekly postal orders

---

13 The distinguished author had been admitted to hospital for a quadruple heart-bypass operation and was mortified to find that while he was there his volume had been published without the extensive proofing he had planned.

14 *Viz.* 'An Inside Job: Reflections on Designs of Academical and Official Dress for the University of the Arts London', *TBS*, 18 (2018), pp. 7–31 (at pp. 15, 16), and 'Chairman's Speech,' *Burgon Sociaty Annual 2001.*

15 The Very Revd Alan Brunskill Webster when Dean of Norwich.

16 8 vols (London: Waverley Book Co., 1955).

17 [s1] Oxford simple shape.

for 7/6d,[18] from the money I earned from my paper round, until I had paid for it, and remember the thrill of it arriving in the post. Inside the parcel was a smart plastic bag with the Ede and Ravenscroft logo in green and gold and inside that the hood itself. I carried it with me everywhere in my school brief case for weeks but lent it one day, reluctantly, to the aforementioned teacher so that his wife could cut a pattern for yet another one of the hoods he wanted her to make for him. In cutting it out she nicked the shot crimson silk of the neckband and although she did a very skilful repair, I remember being distraught at the damage to it. From that time I remember with absolute clarity the look and feel of that hood and others as well: the Wales MA hood of my headmaster, with its glorious green shot blue silk; the Lampeter BA of one of the curates, with its white fur and sealskin spots;[19] the purple lined lilac hood of a Fellow of Trinity College London belonging to one of my aunts, who was the music mistress at my school; the London BSc, with its gold shot white silk; the black piped with blue cord of the Chelmsford diocesan lay-reader's hood; and my absolute favourite: the Diploma in Technology of Loughborough College ([f1], purple Russell cord lined with yellow silk), worn by another of the curates.

A year or two passed and Dr George Shaw's Academical Dress of British Universities was published and my parents gave it to me. I read, learned, marked and inwardly digested it and would not go anywhere without it. Later the same year I began to think about future examinations. In my English class, we were all asked to choose a subject and to begin to write it up as course work that would eventually contribute to a General Certificate of Education exam. I had no hesitation and knew clearly which subject I would choose. With the help of classmates, I wrote to every British university and to every robemaker whose address I could find in directories in the local library, as well as to editors of encyclopaedias. Most of them replied and many of them sent samples, extracts from university calendars, cuttings of silks and helpful descriptions. I still have 'The Degree Hoods of the British Universities' which I first began on 9 October 1966 and have the same frisson of pleasure when looking through the text and admiring the silk cuttings and illustrations.

As a result of one of those letters, Bill Keen, the manager of William Northam & Co., in Star Yard, off Carey Street, London

---

18 Seven shillings and six pence (now 0.38p).
19 The alternative to the ermine tails.

WC2, invited me to work at the shop during my school holidays. Although a separate company with its own history, William Northam, by the 1960s, had links with the much bigger company: Ede & Ravenscroft Ltd and, indeed, the Northam shop was situated at the back of the Chancery Lane premises although it later moved to Fetter Lane and then to Oxford. I enjoyed my holidays working there, dealing with customers, helping at the huge University of London presentation ceremonies in the Albert Hall and learning about fabrics and cutting patterns. It was a complete wonder that anyone would want to pay me for indulging my hobby and for spending my day surrounded by so many gowns and hoods.

After finishing my Ordinary-Level exams, I put on an exhibition of University of London academic dress at school, along with a talk on the Albert Hall ceremonies. I can recall the excitement when the large boxes containing examples of nearly all the London University costumes were delivered to the school from Northam, and can remember the look and feel of the silks and the heavy scarlet superfine wool of the doctors' robes. By the time I was sixteen I had a collection of more than 150 hoods, which sometimes led to a dialogue with my parents!

Amongst the other robemaking companies which replied to me was J. Wippell & Co, from their London headquarters in Tufton Street, London SW1, behind Westminster Abbey. The Managing Director, Mr Michael Wippell also offered me some holiday work and I spent the summer of 1968 (and I think a couple of occasions subsequently) working in the shop and showroom. There were more clerical than academic items there but still a goodly number of gowns, hoods and caps. In my first week there, Michael Wippell gave me a mint copy of the 4th edition of Haycraft & Stringer's The Degree and Hoods of the World's Universities and Colleges, with the words I still remember: 'This is out of print but still obtainable from two dear old ladies in Bath.' I do not know to whom that remark referred, perhaps to relatives of Haycraft himself, but I still have the book.

In 1970, I went up to King's College London to read theology. Lectures were in the fine old buildings next to Somerset House, in the Strand, but those training for the priesthood lived in a grand theological hostel in Vincent Square, Westminster. Gowns were still worn then by professors and many of the students, particularly those reading for degrees in theology, music and, curiously, engineering. Some of us wore our undergraduate gowns whilst walking in the Strand or to and from Vincent Square, through St. James's Park, the Mall and Trafalgar Square.

During this time, I continued to work for various robemaking companies, in the vacations, as well as teaching a bit of Scripture at Westminster Abbey choir school and working as an Abbey guide. Academic and clerical dress was just about everywhere and I did a roaring trade acting as a middleman for Ede & Ravenscroft, Northam, Wippell, Thomas Pratt and James Neal, supplying friends with hoods and gowns, cassocks, surplices, cloaks etc., and also made quite a few hoods for friends, some of which I hear are still being worn fifty years on!

After university, a year's placement at Norwich Cathedral, theological college in Canterbury and ordination, I became curate of a suburban Anglo-Catholic parish, near London, where hoods were definitely not worn in choir; but after four happy years went off to be a public school chaplain where gowns were a daily item of dress. Later, back in a parish as Vicar I lost touch again with the robemaking world. After seven years, I became a Roman Catholic priest and was appointed to a parish in West London. Sadly, this was not an altogether happy experience and I decided to leave and undertake a psychotherapy training programme which required me to experience therapy myself. Soon after I began work as practice counsellor in a busy South London surgery. Then two things happened by way of coincidence: in 1996, during a house move, my school project of 1966 fell out of a bookcase and a friend (now a well-known author) picked it up and didn't laugh at it; and later, the same week, I was walking to collect a watch that had been repaired in Fleet Street, one lunchtime, when I met Bill Keen, the former manager of Northam, who had employed me as a schoolboy. In the meantime, he had become managing director of Ede & Ravenscroft Ltd and he told me that they had been very busy since the time that the polytechnics had received their charters and that Ede & Ravenscroft had grown very quickly to meet the demands, from so many new institutions, of commissions for robes. He asked me what I had been doing since ordination, and whether I might be interested in doing some consultancy for the company which, naturally, I said I most definitely was. We met a few times to discuss how this might work but on the day of the third scheduled meeting I learned that he had died at his desk the week before and that his diary had just said, 'lunch with Philip' and so they hadn't been able to tell me.

Six weeks later, following the funeral, the Chairman of Ede & Ravenscroft asked if I were still interested in some part-time work and I joined the company as Academic Consultant, following up many of Bill Keen's accounts, projects and designs, particularly in connection with the University of London and its numerous colleges and other academic institutions in London and the South East.

From my position in Ede & Ravenscroft I was able to view letters from various like-minded individuals who had written in from time to time. There were some from rather eccentric people and those running bogus institutions as well as those making bona fide enquiries. There were files of letters from Charles Franklyn, George Shaw, Hugh Smith and Nicholas Groves, about whom I had heard as far back as my Northam days but had not yet met. The Ede and Ravenscroft headquarters is at Waterbeach, just outside Cambridge, so during my time at the company I was able to visit Dr Shaw at his house in Grantchester, and various Cambridge robemaking companies, as well as the affable Len Brown of Joshua Taylor & Co, a wholesale robemaker; and Ede & Ravenscroft's own Ron Brookes whose encyclopaedic knowledge of academic dress I eagerly sought. At the time I had no inkling that several of those who were interested in academic dress would one day meet up and form a society for the furtherment and enjoyment of this subject. It was a huge pleasure to meet them, to discover the eGroup and then, together, to found the Burgon Society.

Brother Michael Powell, and the eGroup

The World Wide Web was first made available to the public in 1991 but my time at Ede & Ravenscroft, from 1996, coincided with the growth of the early search engines, many of which have long since disappeared. One of my tasks was to see what references to academic dress were out there and, rather like looking for ET, although there was not a huge amount of information, I made regular searches. In 1999 during a routine search I was thrilled to find that someone called Br Michael Powell,[20] of St George's College, Weybridge, had

20 The Revd Br Dr Michael Powell, FBS, Foundation Fellow, Member of Council then of the Executive Committee (2000–19), co-editor of the

begun an interest group on the subject,[21] and I sent him a message. I will let him begin his story in his own words:

As for the eGroup I started it because I genuinely believed that I might be the only person in the world with such an esoteric interest! I had no previous contact with anyone. It was only when Phil responded (several weeks after the start of the eGroup) that I realised I was not alone. If you remember, at the first meeting in the Wheatsheaf,[22] I was very much against the establishment of a formal group as I preferred to keep things on the hood-fondling level. Time has proven me wrong!

My interest in AD was started by the fact that I didn't have any, having crashed out of Cambridge, and I was singing in church choirs where hoods were de rigueur. I did an ACP,[23] as it seemed to me at the time the easiest way to get a hood (but very boring hood) qualification, followed in fairly short order by the ACertCM.[24] Now, of course, I have hoods by the armful. I suppose the first 'real' hood I got was the MEd (Brunel) when I was about 40, followed immediately by MPhil (Brunel)—same hood—and then the PhD a few years later. I never wear the Brunel masters' hoods as they hang dreadfully.

Having discovered the eGroup, Br Michael and I exchanged email messages before continuing to post on the eGroup itself. We then began to invite others we knew who we thought would be interested to join it. Amongst those I contacted was Nicholas Groves[25] who also knew others with an interest in academic dress. For example, after he discovered Hoodata in 1990, one of the editors, Dr Robin Rees, put him in touch with Professor Hugh Smith and they

first *Annual*; former archivist; examiner for the fellowship.

21 10 July 1999. (At first the group was hosted on the EGroups platform but when this was withdrawn Br Michael moved the academical_dress group to the Yahoo eGroups site).

22 The Wheatsheaf public house in Rathbone Place, London W1.

23 Associate of the College of Preceptors. Founded in 1846 to standardize the teaching profession, it is now known as The Chartered College of Teaching.

24 The Archbishop's Certificate in Church Music.

25 Dr Nicholas Groves, FBS, Foundation Fellow; Director of Research then Dean of Studies (2000–03); Member of Council (2000–12); editor of Shaw III (for which the Burgon Society holds the copyright); drafted the regulations, later the constitution; invented the Groves system for the standardization of terminology for academic dress; author of several Burgon Society publications, examiner for the fellowship.

began a lengthy correspondence which survives. Hugh Smith, or possibly Robin Richardson,[26] introduced Nicholas Groves to Professor (then Doctor) Bruce Christianson.

Dr Nicholas Groves

A quick trawl through my correspondence file shows a letter from Robin[27] dated 6 August 1990, referring to a 'hood chat' we'd had by phone—and we must recall that a good deal of what went on was done by phone. The letter says he'd written to Hugh to suggest me as a collaborator on the (never published) second edition.[28] I rather think that Robin Rees and I got in touch initially via a request for the final number of Hoodata. I then see an initial letter from Hugh dated 21 August 1990—and dozens more after that!

I first came across academic dress, albeit in a nugatory manner, in The Beano—Teacher with his mortar-board, and the Head in cap and gown. This became reality when I went to grammar school where the masters (mostly) wore their gowns every day (caps were never used). Hoods appeared on 1 October, Founder's Day, and I wondered what they might be, then I recalled the table of hoods in the rather aged edition of *Pears' Cyclopaedia* at home: it answered some, but by no means all, questions. Hoods were also worn in the summer for Speech Day, and it is still a matter of annoyance that I never managed to see the hoods of two masters who were with us for a short time only! Then there were hoods being worn in church. I was starting to compile lists, and when I had to do a history project in the second form on a mediæval topic I chose universities, though most of it was about their robes—including an illustrated table of the various gowns worn by the masters! (It still turns up now and then.) Another source was The Congregation in Church—a rather extremely high church little book, explaining what the various ceremonies were about, but it did contain a list of hoods one was likely to see in church, including those of the theological colleges, which was a new addition. I don't recall anyone else at school having more than a passing interest, and I never had the courage to ask the masters about their robes.

On to college in Aberystwyth, and one of the first things I bought was an undergrad gown. They were no longer compulso-

26 Managing Director, J. Wippell & Co. Ltd.
27 Dr Robin Rees.
28 Of Academic Dress and Insignia of the World, Smith and Sheard.

ry at lectures, but my department, Music, required their use for stewarding at concerts, so it got a fair bit of use then, along with organ playing in the vacations. In my second year, a chap doing the one-year postgrad. Diploma in Librarianship got to know of my interest and told me about a book published by his biology master at Lancing: George Shaw. I had access to the National Library of Wales, a copyright library, so while there researching for my dissertation, I also called up what we now know as 'Shaw I', which gave me a great deal of new information. It was a great nuisance that it was published in 1966, as that was a period when many new universities were being founded, but they were not included, so again, I started compiling a manuscript addendum to Shaw, which still exists. This included extending the Hood Key, which is now a BS publication. This was all assisted by later editions of *Pears'*, and university calendars in libraries, which usually contained such information. Also, in the reference section of Norwich library (hunting down their copy of Shaw one day), I came across Degrees and Hoods—the fifth (1972) edition, and the notoriously eccentric work by Dr Franklyn, Academical Dress... . I think there was a copy of Hargreaves-Mawdsley there, too. It was at this time that I had the idea of the hood and gown codes. They are less than logical, as all I had to rely on was Shaw, and he does not include several patterns, so additions have been stuck on the end. They are now so well known that it would be impossible to revise them!

On a visit to Cambridge in 1976, I went to Heffers bookshop to see if I could get a copy of Shaw, but this was not possible. However, they did give me George's address, so I wrote to him, and he kindly sent me a copy: it is dated August 1976. Also, I was able to gain access to the Cambridge University library, via a friend who was a BA, and there I found Hugh Smith's work. The library service at home provided the British Library lending copy—several times! (I eventually acquired a set via abe.com in 2017.)

My own first set of robes was my BMus set from Ede's in 1977—gown £20.00, hood £12.00, as I recall. I already had a square, which I'd bought in the annual clearance sale at the college outfitters in Aber for £1.00! (It now seems to be lost.) This set was to be joined by many others over the years. (I think I am entitled to about 30 hoods, though I don't have half of them.) I also started collecting hoods and, to a lesser extent, gowns. My first purchase was during the Long Vac of 1975, an Oxford BMus from an antique shop (it's still with me). I recall they also had the habit and hood for the Oxford DD, but my purse would not run to it. My particular interest is the Anglican theological colleges and the music colleges, as well as developments at the universities in the later C19.

Having a visual mind, I started to draw and colour in the hoods for every university and college, a project that started on loose sheets of paper in 1978; was redone in an A5 sketch-book in 1990; and then in an A4 one in 1991, which is the one still in use, with many, many additions, corrections, and extra pages stuck in. It does reveal how vague some descriptions are: I have often cheerfully drawn a hood in line with what I think it meant, only to find out some time later, on seeing an example, that it's nothing like that!

Also, I was writing to robemakers and universities for information. This was an era when universities actually knew about their own AD, and robemakers gladly shared information. The correspondence file still exists and is of use. The first item in is a response from M. T. O'Regan of Ryder & Amies dated 8 February 1978, giving me information on the recently introduced Cambridge degrees of MPhil and BEd. He also sent me a copy of the old Almond booklet on the graduates' robes. There are letters from Northam (signed by Bill Keen), Joshua Taylor (signed by Len Brown), Shepherd & Woodward (signed by J. R. Venables), and a large number of universities and colleges, including one from the Assistant Registrar at Leicester, Cliff Dunkley, whom I later got to know via the Burgon Society. Ridley of Norwich let me see the UEA robes.

I had also got to know the late Denis Puxty, of the Guild of Church Musicians, and he provided me with a set of copies of Hoodata, all except the last one, so I wrote to Robin Rees to ask for a copy, and that was the start of my association with him. He was in touch with Hugh Smith and suggested to him that I might help with revising his magnum opus, and I have my first letter from Hugh dated 21 August 1990. He thought that George's second edition was 'something of a disappointment', and that the 1972 Degrees and Hoods ('Haycraft 5') was 'an unmitigated disaster'! He also thought that my hood and gown codes were too simplified and did not distinguish enough among versions of (say) [f1], though that is rather the point! Anyway, we had a long and useful collaboration until his death, and I have a set of the revisions for the entries for the UK and Irish robes. My last letter from him is dated 30 October 1997.

I have a feeling I was put in touch with Bruce Christianson via Robin Richardson at Wippell (first surviving letter from Bruce is 14 April 1994), and possibly with Stephen James also, and Phil got in touch with me. This was just before the start of the internet; alas, the letters do not survive. Then the internet came, but those e-mails are long gone—two computers and two e-mail addresses ago!—and Phil told me about the eGroup, to which I signed up. I think I may have made the first posts—about the Lampeter hoods, of course, on which I was writing at the time. I did indeed add Matthew and Giles; one of them added Ian Elliot-Davies. I was at the Wheatsheaf meeting.

Dr Giles Brightwell

Another of those who joined the eGroup and came along to the meetings was Giles Brightwell.[29] He knew Nicholas Groves from living in Norwich but also Dr John Horton from his time as an undergraduate at Sidney Sussex College, Cambridge. Dr Brightwell writes:

I first became interested in academic dress when I was in the choir at prep school (Orwell Park in Suffolk) where we wore blue gowns rather than cassocks and surplices. Gowns, I gather, were thought to be more practical and less Catholic for a low-church school/parish than the alternative. That said, we used Percy Dearmer's Songs of Praise, which can hardly be said to be a low-church hymnal.

At Harrow, all the masters wore gowns and many in those days (1984-88) wore mortar boards too. On Speech Day and at Churchill Songs hoods were worn by most of the masters as well as the senior boys who had achieved music diplomas from the Royal Schools/RCO. Doctoral dress robes and hats were worn by those who were entitled to them—I think there were five altogether including a London PhD in Science, a St Andrews PhD in French, and several Oxford DPhils. Added to that, a life-size portrait of Professor Sir Percy Buck (director of music for 26 years) dressed in court dress and his Oxford DMus robes, adorned the wall of the main corridor in the Music Department. Buck had held his Harrow post concurrently with that of professor of composition at the RCM, King Edward VII Professor of Music at King's, London, and

---

29 Giles Brightwell, FBS, Foundation Fellow; Member of Council (2000–02).

Trinity, Dublin (I think), alongside being HM Inspector of Music in Schools. He was giant of a man. In the careers department, there were prospectuses from each university and so I much enjoyed thumbing through those to find pictures of the various robes at each university. Many of the masters who were Oxford or Cambridge MAs had still retained their BA gowns and undergraduate gowns. Some were kind enough to allow me to borrow them so that in the holidays from school, I could have a gown to wear as I played the organ in North Essex for church services. My first gown was an altered Cambridge BA gown (made without strings and with the slits in the sleeve left open at the bottom), made by Ede & Ravenscroft in Cambridge.

My parents had a copy of *Pears' Cyclopaedia*, which listed the university hoods' colours. I particularly loved the description of the Sheffield Arts crushed strawberry lining, which, for me, was redolent of perfect English summers.

As a teenager, I spent a year in Norwich in 1989–90 as a choral scholar at the Cathedral where I met Nick Groves—need I say more? He sparked my interest and I loved looking through his hand-drawn and hand-coloured hood book. In those carefree days I had a hood run up for each diploma I had been given along with a few more that I (and others) had invented! I wore them all at Norwich in daily rotation until the organist, Michael Nicholas, suggested that I lock a particularly beautiful creation (Cambridge shape: Medici crimson, lined silver taffeta, bound 1" and part-lined 6" white fur) in a cupboard and throw away the key! I think he felt it looked too much like the Cambridge MusB—perish the thought!

Having spent several years catching up, academically speaking, after a fairly challenging time at Harrow, I went to Durham as a mature student in 1991. I felt fortunate to be at a university where, in the 1990s at least, gowns were regularly worn by undergraduates. Gray and Son made the Durham scholar's gowns long and full without being specifically requested to do so: I was delighted. Along with my friends, I wore my gown and mortar board to Evensong in the cathedral each day because the university regulations recommended we do so.

At the end of my first year, I was invited to play for graduation ceremonies in the Castle Great Hall at Durham, which I continued to do for eight years. Sir Peter Ustinov was Chancellor and it was enormous fun to play for the recipients of *honoris causa* degrees as well as earned ones. I loved the robe-and people-spotting. As you know, I followed that with a similar post at the University of Glasgow.

I have always harboured an ambition to earn a Durham DMus and have been eligible to submit for several years now but finding the time is always a challenge.

I don't remember much about the Yahoo group but I suppose I was a member. My prime contact has always been Nick G. and through him I got to know others. Thank you, Nick.

Dr Robin Rees

Robin Rees,[30] who took over as editor of Hoodata from Squadron Leader Alan Birt, was another active member of the eGroup. Dr Rees writes:

When I was about ten years old, my headmaster began wearing some strange black-and-red garb at the school's annual prize-giving. In contrast, my own attire on those occasions (e.g., a patterned table cloth as an Wise Man in the Nativity Play, or gold and white silk as in angel) made a mere MA (Oxon) look distinctly drab.

At Westminster School, I soon noticed that some boys (Queen's Scholars, whose role is to proclaim 'Vivat' at Coronations) were wearing in lessons a full-length black gown. Though not envious, I was certainly interested. An event that truly kindled my fascination with academic dress was the installation of Dr Eric Abbott as Dean of Westminster. There were probably at least 150 clergy present with relatively few wearing the same design of what I later learned was a hood.

Seemingly insignificant comments can have profound long-term consequences. One day at lunch, my housemaster Dr Haines casually mentioned that in addition to his everyday black gown, he also had a red one for special occasions.

In due course, I acquired the dress for a London undergraduate and, later, a BSc (whose hood, like my earlier angelic costume, features the colours gold and white). At our graduation ceremony in the Royal Albert Hall, the Chancellor customarily places the hood over the head of each of the Higher Doctors. That day, the Queen Mother managed to put every hood on back-to-front.

---

30 Dr Robin Rees, FBS, Foundation Fellow; Member of Council (2000–02), died 2021.

Part-time research in ionospheric physics led to a London MPhil, whose hood had no fewer than four colours (black, claret, white and gold). I confess that I was not enamoured by this, but felt consoled when the University agreed to my proposal of adding a 1-inch claret facing to the black Master's gown.

Later, I encountered Hoodata, an occasional newsletter featuring hoods, and its founding editor: Sqn Ldr Alan Birt (later FBS). On reading in Hoodata about the introduction of academic dress for qualifications at the Royal Institute of Chemistry, I managed, albeit with difficulty, to persuade my own Institute of Physics to do likewise. Was my stipulation that the hood be 1 metre long a consequence of my sense of scientific precision—or my sense of humour? We shall never know. The Institute of Biology followed suit with, I believe, the encouragement of Dr George Shaw (later FBS).

On succeeding Alan as editor, I got to know him, Dr Nicholas Groves (later FBS), and several others who shared our common interest.

Life is a strange thing. Nineteen years after failing to get into Oxford as an undergraduate, I accepted the offer of a job there. This brought with it MA Status (including the right to wear the gown and hood) and an invitation to the annual Encaenia Garden Party (a truly colourful gathering), both privileges continuing to this day. Before retiring from Oxford, I completed a PhD in my spare time. I wonder whether Dr Haines unwittingly played a part in this, and whether Sheffield as my choice of University was at all influenced by its PhD gown and hood ...

Here ... I should draw to a close. Suffice it to say that I gratefully accepted the opportunity to become a Foundation Fellow of the Burgon Society. I greatly value my involvement in it, and the friendships made.

Meeting up

On the eGroups academical_dress site the earliest messages available, from 15 to 17 September 1999, show members assisting Nicholas Groves in his questions about the robes for St David's College, Lampeter and for the revisions he was compiling to the second edition of Shaw.

On 23 September 1999, I wrote to the group as follows:

> I wonder whether members would like to meet in order to plan how we might proceed as a group? It would be possi-

ble for me to arrange a simple working lunch here at Chancery Lane, although I should want to keep the company out of such gatherings.

We might join the Costume Society, as a group. We could arrange talks, visits etc. The main object, as I see it, is to foster interest in our unusual area of knowledge. Please let us have some debate about this. Members may have very different suggestions. I shall resist the temptation to design academical dress for membership of our society (if there is one)!

The first reply came 30 minutes later from Giles Brightwell:

"Phil, I'd be happy to meet at Chancery Lane sometime as part of a newly formed interest group."

And, a little later, from Timothy Milner:[31]

I should certainly be interested in a meeting. Friday lunchtime or sometime in the evening would be best for me. I am currently a student in heraldic painting and calligraphy at Reigate School of Art. I have been encouraging the correct wearing of academical dress at Cambridge University (of which I am an MA) in recent times and have spoken in University Discussions on several occasions. I am also an MA in the University of Wales (Aberystwyth).

The same afternoon, John Horton wrote:

I should certainly like to be at such a meeting if at all possible. With members spread around the country though, it is inevitable that no time will suit everyone. It might be best to arrange a time that suits a few at least—and then report back via a thread to this eGroup—rather than struggle to find a time that suits everyone.

And, also, Timothy Cutts:[32]

It would be rather a long way for me to travel from Aberystwyth to Chancery Lane in order to attend a working lunch. However, if a meeting is arranged, I look forward to hearing the outcome of the discussions.

---

31 Timothy Milner, FBS, a member of the eGroup didn't attend the meetings but has followed the progress of the Society with interest. He later became one of the Proctors in the University of Cambridge.

32 Timothy Cutts was a member of the eGroup but distance prevented him from attending the meetings and, later, we rather lost touch with him.

Meanwhile, Br Michael had returned from the USA to find the group up and running and he and I corresponded by email for some days. Later, he posted on the eGroup:

> Greetings. I am delighted to find that my establishing this group has met with so much response. I have been away for two weeks in California and was happy to see that there had been activity in my absence. I have been communicating by e-mail with Phil since my return. I am putting the more important points of our communications here in the public forum.
>
> I have been fascinated by academic dress for years, ever since I came across a copy of Haycraft in a second-hand book-shop. I started the eGroup as I hoped I might find others who shared what must be a rather arcane interest.
>
> I have the usual books (and have ordered Phil's),[33] but would be interested in any others. My last acquisition was a book on American Academic Heraldry (Sheard) which I found through www.bibliofind.com. I have for a long time been trying to get a copy of the 'limited edition' Shaw book but with no success.
>
> I have over the years collected a number of diplomas etc. with academic dress. Some are a bit 'mickey mouse' but it amuses me. I have an MEd and an MPhil from Brunel (same hood) and am currently working full time on a Doctorate, also at Brunel. Other than that I have six other hoods.
>
> Phil mentioned the possibility of a warehouse tour—this sounds fascinating.
>
> You might be interested in the various diplomas I mentioned:
>
> College of Preceptors (associate)—Purple lined Purple, special simple shape
>
> Guild of Musicians and Singers (fellow)—Maroon lined and edged Purple, Glasgow shape
>
> Northern and Midland School of Music (Member)—Sea Green lined Old Gold, Burgon
>
> Victoria College of Music (fellow)—Royal Blue lined Scarlet edged Fur, simple
>
> Academy of St Cecilia (fellow)—Royal Blue lined and edged Gold, cowl edged inside 3" pink, Glasgow shape.
>
> Guild of Church Musicians (Archbishop's Certificate)—Black lined black, cowl edged 1" Royal Blue edged with Terra Cotta cord, simple.

---

33 P. Goff, *University of London Academic Dress* (London: University of London Press, 1999).

If anyone has information on any other societies etc. with academic dress I would be interested to hear.

As for the idea of a meeting which has been proposed I am not against the idea, but I would hate things to become too formalised. I live near London so travel would not be a problem.

Later the same day, Nicholas Groves responded to the message and suggested a possible name for the future society.

I would be happy to attend a meeting in London, as it's just under two hours on the train for me (!!). As far as I am aware, my teaching commitments this term would indicate that Monday or Thursday would be possible (tho' other days may be available if classes don't run ...)

Perhaps members might like to bring along some hoods (certainly 'the rarer birds' for display. I have a collection, some of which I am entitled to (and some of which are, as Michael says, rather Mickey Mouse!), and others which I have inherited or bought. The list is too long to post here, but perhaps we could all post lists of what we possess?

I have just finished compiling a list of corrigenda (and addenda) to Shaw's 1995 volume; I can e-mail to anyone who would like a copy.

Some time ago, some friends and I tried setting up an academic dress society (which never got off the ground), but we were going to call it the Burgon Society, as Dean B is the only person to have had a hood shape named after him. Perhaps we could use this name?

The next day, 24 September, I replied to the group and part of the message is as follows:

Thanks for all the comments so far, I especially like Nick's suggestion about Dean Burgon, and Michael's that we don't get too formal. It was also very interesting to realise that our fascination with this subject is a shared thing. Perhaps other members could say a little about themselves in relation to academic dress as a hobby.

I concluded the message by saying:

The other thing which occupies my mind is whether it would be possible to have a permanent display of academic dress (permanent but changing often!) somewhere in the UK, perhaps within an existing museum or academic institution. If we were a group or society we would have more strength and clout!

The following week, Matthew Duckett sent a message by way of an introduction, part of which reads:

> Greetings to list members—some of whom are already friends of mine (small world ...)
>
> An introduction: I currently work at UCL where I'm the deputy superintendent of the Physiology Department. I've been interested in academic dress and related 'tat' really since my graduation in 1985 (BSc, East Anglia); since then I have acquired a few more bits and pieces in addition—notably the Royal Society of Chemistry (CChem, MRSC—but the hood is the same as for GRSC, grey stuff fully lined with purple silk) and a few diplomas including one from the Norwich School of Church Music (thanks, Nick!). I'm also supposed to be writing up a PhD thesis at Birkbeck College, but that if not dead is at least sleeping. I also have a PGCE from East Anglia ... .

The Revd Matthew Duckett[34]

Apart from a hazy childhood background of black and white films and the Molesworth books, my first impression of academic dress probably came from morning assembly in the Grammar School I attended, where the Headmaster and his Deputy would breeze in in black gowns (not worn at any other time in the school day) and, so attired, conduct the proceedings. Mysterious proceedings they were, too; nothing was ever explained, including the attire of the officiants. The hymns were deadly, the prayers devoid of sincerity. The summoning to the stage of the third under-fifteens (or whoever it might be) to receive 'colours' might as well have been a Masonic initiation for all I knew what was going on. And then there were the notices, mostly forgotten, but occasionally sparking curious memories, such as the time the Headmaster sternly warned the School against the new 'head-shaking music', which might cause brain damage and seriously impair a boy's prospects in the City.

But those gowns intrigued me. The Headmaster, I was to come to learn, was an Oxford DPhil, though I didn't at that stage know anything of the distinctive dress of different institutions.

The university I happened to choose—for the course and the city it was in—was East Anglia; only when I was there did I discover its academic dress: Cecil Beaton's lurid designs channelling

---

34 Matthew Duckett, FBS, Foundation Fellow; Member of Council (2000–01) Membership Secretary; Treasurer.

the pure spirit of the 60s in vibrant slabs and space-age folds of shimmering polyester. I was admittedly pleased with the Spectrum Green of my BSc, but rather envied the Magenta of Laws. If only I had seen a catalogue of hoods before choosing my A-levels!

What was it about academic dress that fascinated? I think partly the idea of something that you had to earn the right to wear, a mark of distinction. But also the rich colours and quality fabrics in an age of dullness and bad style.

I returned to UEA two years after graduation to take my PGCE. My religious opinions in the years away had developed in a distinctly Anglo-Catholic direction, so I didn't return to the chaplaincy worship in which, even before, I had been an awkward fit. Instead, I sought out the most 'advanced' church in the city (of Norwich), where, by great good fortune, I met Nick Groves who was at the time the Director of Music. Knowing there was keen competition with the serving team, he got in first and asked if I would like to join the choir. Nick explained that the custom was for graduates to wear their hoods in choir. Did I have my hood? 'Oh, yes', I said. His eyes lit up ...

Wearing a UEA hood over a surplice is tricky, as anyone knows who has tried it. The neckband is too wide to fit under the surplice neatly, and the material too slippery to stay in place on the shoulders. But it was the envy in the 'green' seasons of those who liked their hoods to match liturgical colours!

Green was soon supplemented by the rather splendid cerise of the Norwich School of Church Music, then very much a flourishing concern. Through this and other Colleges and Guilds, and some rather more obscure and transitory organisations (let the reader understand!), I met many kindred souls.

Academic dress, it turned out, was a subject of study and research in its own right, and there were lots of people interested in studying it seriously. I forget who it was who first approached me about being involved in starting the Burgon Society to take part in organising such work, but I was certainly a willing volunteer. I don't think at the time I foresaw the level of interest that the Society would so quickly attract, or that it would grow to be the authoritative body in the field, with a level of serious academic discipline and quality research recognised around the world.

It's a matter of regret that, due to growing personal commitments and responsibilities, I wasn't able to devote longer to active participation in the work of the Society. But I was there at the beginning, and it is remarkable to see how far it has come in the years since. Long may it continue: Floreat Burgon!

On the eGroup, discussion took place about robes for the musical colleges and Stephen James raised the question of why so many who were interested in academic dress were also musically inclined. At the time, Nicholas Groves was working on a booklet describing the robes of the music colleges and societies and this was later published by the Burgon Society.[35] Br Michael, meanwhile had opened a 'vault' on the eGroup website for sharing photographs and illustrations of various items of academic dress.

On 28 September 1999, Br Michael wrote as follows:

> We now have 12 members of the group,[36] and there has been some exchange of ideas that we should a) meet and b) consider forming an Association. Experience suggests that unless a specific proposal is made nothing happens. May I, therefore, make a specific proposal?
>
> 1. I propose that all interested meet informally in London at a time and place TBA but in early November. Perhaps we could take up Phil's earlier offer re. Chancery Lane? Alternatively, I have friends who run a pub just off Oxford St. who might help.
>
> 2. The formation of an Association could be a point of discussion but would not be the principal goal of such a meeting.
>
> In the meantime, could we all encourage anyone else we know to be interested to at least subscribe to the eGroup.

The next day I sent a message to the members:

> Just a quick message to thank Nick for uploading the music info and the corrections to Dr Shaw's last book (which are excellent—I have been pencilling corrections in for ages but not in the systematic way Nick and Hugh have done). The info is most helpful.
>
> About meeting, I have no special feelings other than it would be great to see you all sometime. Perhaps so as to prevent too much of E&R entering into our domain we should let Michael arrange the meeting at the pub and then I will offer some

---

35 Nicholas Groves and John Kersey, *Academical Dress of Music Colleges and Societies of Musicians in the United Kingdom* (London: Burgon Society, 2002).

36 Of which eleven went on to be the founders.

dates for a trip to the warehouse in Cambridge. I have to say that I find the warehouse very tedious, and after seeing the first 10,000 gowns I glaze over. I do, however, have some interesting archive pieces both in London and Cambridge.

If any members would like to call in at Chancery Lane just phone me to make a time and I will arrange a simple break-fast/lunch/tea/after work pint (delete as appropriate). I would prefer individual visits or a max of four because space is very limited. Whilst most robes are in Cambridge, I keep my archive of books, illustrations etc in London. It is important to phone first and make a time since I look after the contracts for all the London universities and colleges, amongst other things, and therefore am in and out of them all the time.

My last suggestion is that we have an annual dinner at a club or large hotel which would be preceded by a reception. We would, of course, all wear academic dress. Wouldn't it be fun— like the Masons without the boring bits (apols to any Masons)! It a great pity to see what was once the ordinary daily dress of scholars and clerics consigned to graduation ceremonies only where it is often worn by people who wouldn't know what ac-ademic dress was if it jumped up and bit them. There are very few schools now where academic dress is worn on a daily basis and that leaves the clergy and Church organists (hmm there seems to be a connection with our group here ...)

2
Burgeoning Burgon

The account of the stages which mark the Burgon Society's birth and early existence is rather detailed and therefore it might be a good idea to keep in mind the following summary.

As is common with such groups, the Burgon Society came gradually into formal existence. There was a preliminary meeting of interested members of the Academic Dress eGroup at the Wheatsheaf public house in Rathbone Place, off Oxford Street, London, in November 1999; and a second meeting at the University of London Chaplaincy in June 2000. At the second meeting, the decision to form the society was taken in principle, and the original members became Foundation Fellows of the Burgon Society with effect from the beginning of August 2000. Further meetings were held in September and October of that year, at the University of London Chaplaincy and Senate House respectively. At the September meeting (referred to on the agenda as the Inaugural Meeting of the Burgon Society) officers were appointed, and the Society's constitution and academic dress were discussed in detail. At the October meeting the officers and constitution were formally ratified, and the Society's first fellowship examination was conducted. The meeting on 21 of October 2000 was from then on regarded as the official Foundation Day for the Burgon Society, and the Society has thenceforth celebrated its birthdays by holding a Congregation each October for the admission of new fellows.

The Wheatsheaf meeting

In the year before the Society's founding, others discovered the eGroup independently and the number of members began to grow. It soon seemed a good idea for us to meet up and, as mentioned previously, Br Michael suggested the Wheatsheaf public house, in Rathbone Place, off Oxford Street, London, because he knew the owner and it had a back room where we could meet. The first meeting of eGroup members took place on 13 November 1999 and, apart from myself, comprised Br Michael Powell; Nicholas Groves (who also invited Giles Brightwell, Matthew Duckett and Stephen James), and The Revd Ian Elliot Davies.

Dr Nicholas Groves writes:

The Wheatsheaf meeting was, IIRC, Michael, me, Phil, and I think Matthew (Duckett). The priest was Ian Elliot Davies. There was also Stephen James—he bought his vicar's Lampeter BA hood, which we discovered was full of hay!

The Revd Canon Dr Stephen James[37]

My initial (and to be honest tentative) interest started, like many others, by noticing the gowns, and on speech days, the hoods worn by the teachers at school. Around the same time I noticed that the *Pears' Cyclopaedia*, which I was given each year, included a section on Academic Dress.

My interest was further kindled when I realised the diplomas I was awarded as a music student each had a different hood.

In the 1980s, while studying part time for a MA degree, I came across books by George Shaw and Smith & Sheard in the library at Reading University, from which I got a much wider view of the subject.

In 1990, I wrote to Ede & Ravenscroft, expressing my interest in AD and asking if it might be possible to visit their premises to look at the various gowns and hoods. Although they were unable to host a visit, they did send me a list of some books about AD and other types of uniform.

Although I can't remember how it happened, in 1992, I found out about Nicholas Groves and exchanged several letters. This subsequently led to contact with John Horton and George Shaw.

In 2000, Nick (Groves) invited me to attend the first meeting of what subsequently became the Burgon Society. I attended each of the meetings and was very pleased to be elected a foundation fellow and the society's first registrar and a few years later to succeed Phil Goff as chairman.

---

37 Dr Stephen James, FBS, Foundation Fellow; Member of Council (2000–07); Registrar; second Chairman.

Br Michael Powell recalls those early days.

My memory is that I started the first newsgroup and then heard nothing for months until Phil popped up, then others slowly joined it.

The first actual informal gathering was in a back room of the Wheatsheaf in Rathbone Place but I can't exactly remember who was there. We were about 7, I think. There was an Anglican priest there who soon disappeared. All I remember about him was that he brought along a Warham hood and it was the first one I had seen.[38]

It hadn't been possible for all those who were interested to come to the meeting but we continued to share information on the eGroup and later the same day, on the evening of 13 November, Br Michael posted a message:

> Just returned from London after a very successful first meeting. We were seven, and a fine array of academic regalia was in evidence to be shown around and admired (or not in some cases). I think there must have been 20 hoods in circulation. Stars of show were Ian's Warham Guild hood and the now superseded Norwich Society hood. (Please get this society up and running again asap with an option for the original hood—I want one!!).[39] Prize for the 'academic dress most likely to make one lunge for the sunglasses' was a complete Leeds doctoral fig. The landlord of the Wheatsheaf was very welcoming, and as we were unable to use the originally planned room, we were given sandwiches as a peace offering. I will be writing to John to thank him on our behalf. Quite what his regulars must have thought I dread to think!
>
> There was much general discussion but a few points came up:
>
> 1. There was a question of scanning Hoodata to go in the vault. The state of existing copies makes this non-feasible.
>
> 2. Philip was quite keen that we should act as a pressure group for the establishment of some form of academic dress museum or dept. of an existing institute. We would have more clout if we were a formal society (at least in name) and perhaps affiliated to the Costume Society. No decision was taken on this

38 The Revd Ian Elliot Davies, then assistant curate of All Saints' Church, Margaret Street, London W1, brought along his Wales BD hood made up in this shape.

39 This was the Norwich School of Church Music. The original fellowship hood was [f1] medici crimson lined silver.

matter. It was felt that we did not want to become too formal in ourselves.

    3. Future meetings—with the next one being in late January–February 2000. Possibly–

    a) a visit to E&R's Fenland warehouse. This was felt to be a good idea but perhaps not until the Spring as the weather in the Fens can be hideous in the winter.

    b) a visit to the Law Courts' legal dress exhibit followed perhaps by a visit to Chancery Lane.

    c) a formal dinner later in 2000 which would be full fig. It was suggested that members should wear different academic dress for each course!

    d) Members with contact addresses for various academic dress awarding bodies, however arcane, should post them. (I have information for: Victoria College of Music, Guild of Church Musicians, Academy of St Cecilia, Guild of Musicians and Singers, Northern and Midlands School of Music and will post them in due course.)

    Perhaps members who were present could add anything they feel I have omitted, and all members are invited to comment.

The First Chaplaincy meeting

The second meeting of eGroup members took place at the University of London Chaplaincy in Gordon Square London WC1 on 17 June 2000. (The university chaplain was my contemporary at Kings College London and I sometimes rented a room there to see clients in my psychotherapy practice.) Those present were: Giles Brightwell, Bruce Christianson, Peter Durant, Nicholas Groves, Philip Goff, John Horton, and Stephen James.

    Nicholas Groves advertised the meeting to members of the eGroup as follows:

From: Nicholas Groves <nwgroves@u...>
Date: Tue Jun 13, 2000 7:52pm
Subject: The Meeting.!!!

For those who are coming on Saturday, we have obtained (through Phil Goff's good offices) the use of the University Chaplaincy Office, at 48b, Gordon Square (near Malet Street). It will be open for us from 1100, so I suggest that we have an informal meeting (doubtless involving the waving of hoods at each other, as last time!), and adjourn to a nearby hostelry for lunch in due course. At present I am expecting seven; if anyone else is intending to come, can you let me know, please? Likewise if you will be arriving significantly after 1100. Nick.

We had a lively discussion and, again, some brought along hoods to admire. At the meeting, at the risk of being a killjoy, I raised again the question of whether we might form a society for the enjoyment of but also the study of academic dress. There was little resistance to this idea but since Br Michael, who had begun the academic dress eGroup, was not present at the meeting, there was concern that he should be fully on-board with the idea. My own thinking was that if we wanted to have any influence or standing in this particular field of costume then we needed to complement our enjoyment of the actual costumes with solid research into their history and development or we wouldn't be taken seriously. With this two-fold objective, we might seek affiliation with existing well-established bodies within the costume and dress world. However, there was also another reason for wanting to balance the fun we were having with some gravity. At the time, a group called the CIL, Central Institute of London, was also in existence and was principally involved with lots of dressing-up at ceremonies at which all kinds of awards were being made. We made a conscious decision to ensure that whatever we started would be taken seriously. That this was the right decision was borne out, in some measure later, by the CIL folding-up its operation and giving way to the Burgon Society. We, in turn, could afford to be gracious and promptly made the very affable Provost of CIL a Fellow of the Society, *honoris causa*.[40]

On the eGroup Nicholas Groves had suggested that we name the group after the only person to have a hood associated with his name—the irascible nineteenth century clergyman, John Burgon, who was an upholder of all things traditional in the University of Oxford, including, so it was said, its dress.[41]

Several of those present at this second meeting have written about what they remember of the event and also how they first became involved with academic dress. Amongst them was Peter Durant,[42] who upon Googling 'academic dress' found the eGroup and saw the meeting advertised there.

40 Stephen Callender Grant, FBS, a registered nurse and nursing historian.

41 The Very Revd John William Burgon, MA, BD (1813–88). A pre-Tractarian high churchman, he graduated from Worcester College, Oxford in 1841 and was elected to a fellowship of Oriel College in 1846. In 1863 he was made vicar of the University Church of St Mary the Virgin. In 1867 he became Gresham Professor of Divinity and Dean of Chichester in 1876.

42 Peter Durant, FBS, Foundation Fellow; Member of Council; (2000–17) Webmaster.

Peter Durant

I first became interested in academic dress as a young grammar school boy. The headmaster and his teaching staff would wear their gowns for morning assembly and often for teaching as well, particularly during the winter if the boiler was broken! By the third form, I could distinguish among the shapes of the Oxford, Cambridge and London gowns, which represented the three institutions from which a majority of staff hailed. Hoods only appeared on Speech Day, so my recognition skills here did not go much beyond the black and crimson of an Oxford MA.

My interest in the subject was maintained at university. This was assisted by the fact that my Professor as well as most other members of the Theology Department at Exeter routinely wore their gowns for teaching, and in the case of the former, with the addition of his mortar board. One of my first tasks as an undergraduate was to find out what academic dress I would be entitled to wear when I graduated. It was whilst engaged on this search that I first came across George Shaw's *Academical Dress of British Universities*. Thereafter, I spent a great deal of my time in the Library when I should have been writing essays, instead studying this tome, and looking for pictures of the robes it described in copies of the various university prospectuses which the Library possessed. Being too impatient to wait until graduation, I decided to purchase an undergraduate gown from Wippell's, but was disappointed that not many of my fellow undergraduates followed my example.

After graduation, my exposure to academic dress was limited, apart from a brief period when I lived and worked in Oxford. Just before the turn of the Millennium, however, I enrolled on an evening class at the City University. Here I reacquainted myself with Shaw's *Academical Dress* as well as Hargreaves-Mawdsley's *History of Academical Dress*, both of which were in the University Library. By now, the internet had become more prevalent, and this led to my discovery of the newly created Academic Dress eGroup. I had missed the first meeting that subscribers to the group had arranged, but duly attended the second meeting on 17 June 2000 at the Chaplaincy Rooms in Gordon Square. It was here that the idea of forming the Burgon Society was proposed—by Philip Goff, as I recall—and subsequently taken forward.

Another of those present at the second meeting in Gordon Square was Professor Bruce Christianson,[43] who had previously met Nicholas Groves perhaps via Robin Richardson of J. Wippell & Co. However, Bruce had also found the eGroup independently, through a routine search, and his first message to the group was dated January 2000. Here is what he has written about his introduction to academic dress.

Professor Bruce Christianson

I'm from New Zealand, and I first encountered academic dress at the age of four when I started school. The staff wore gowns to assembly, and hoods on special occasions. I was instantly fascinated: the gowns had different sleeves, and the hoods had different coloured linings. Most of the hoods had a white fur trim, as well as a pretty coloured silk lining, but the hoods of the people wearing the batman sleeves didn't have any fur. What could it all mean?

Most of the finery on display was from the (now disbanded) federal University of New Zealand, so the gowns were basically Cambridge, albeit colonial fashion lagged a generation or two behind, so the sleeve of the bachelors' gown still came down to the wrist as it did at Cambridge in the 1930s. The hoods were Cambridge MA shape, with a pink lining for Arts degrees and blue for Science degrees, along with the very occasional bright orange of a degree in Commerce. The bachelors' hoods also had a white fur trim inside the edge of the cowl, whereas the masters' hoods did not.

At the age of eight I discovered the first edition of Shaw in the Auckland Central Library, along with a copy of Hargreaves-Mawdsley. A few years later I came across the three volumes of Smith for the first time, and for me Hugh has been the gold standard ever since.

By the time I was an undergraduate at the Victoria University of Wellington, I had also met Scobie-Stringer, *Pears' Cyclopaedia*, and the works of Charles Franklyn. I was genuinely convinced that Franklyn was a made-up character, like Monty Python or Dr Bert Fegg, and I remember thinking that his clearly ironic ranting was hilarious.

43 Professor Bruce Christianson, FBS, Foundation Fellow; second Dean of Studies/Director of Research (2003–16); member of Council (2000–10) then of the Executive Committee (2010–16); examiner and mentor of candidates for the fellowship; member of the editorial board: Transactions of the Burgon Society.

When I graduated, I rented my gown but bought my hood (as was customary) from the New Zealand Federation of University Women as it then was. It came in the form of pre-cut pieces of silk, cloth, and fur, together with a sheet of sewing directions. One crucial step involved turning the whole confection inside out through the hole at the end of the liripipe lining. The fur was then set so as to be removable on promotion to a master's degree.

I moved to England to do my doctorate, and I couldn't honestly say that Oxford's DPhil dressing gown wasn't a factor in my choice of institution. When I started lecturing at the Hatfield Polytechnic, before it became the University of Hertfordshire, the academic dress for students was mostly CNAA and BTEC, with a smattering of University of London external students. The new education bill giving us university status (and abolishing the CNAA!) was implemented in a great hurry, and I found myself part of a group charged with writing a complete set of academic regulations in three months. Of course, the most important of these was the regulation specifying the university's academic dress, which we needed to design first,[44] and that was how (in 1991) I met Robin Richardson.[45]

Hugh Smith had written enquiring about our academic dress to our Registrar, who passed Hugh's letter to me, and so we started corresponding. I also found myself writing to George Shaw to defend some of our decisions. A little while later I made contact with Hugh's collaborator Nick Groves, who, like George and Mary Shaw, was a guest at one of our early award ceremonies.

One day, a routine search turned up the Yahoo group, and I was delighted to meet such a large number of other aficionados online, and later (in many cases) in person. I wasn't at the Wheatsheaf meeting, but made it to the next meeting, in Gordon Square.

Dr John Horton

Also present at the second meeting was Dr John Horton[46] with whom I had made contact in the late 1990s, whilst at Ede & Ravenscroft, as he relates:

---

44 See, Bruce Christianson and Brian Piggott, Academic Dress in the University of Hertfordshire, 1st edn (Hatfield: University of Hertfordshire, 1993).

45 Managing Director of J. Wippell & Co., clerical and academic robemaker.

46 Dr John Horton, FBS, member of Council; Marshal (2000–).

I first met academical dress in 1972 when I moved to grammar school in a small market town on the Welsh border. The headmaster wore a gown at morning assembly and that was it ... except for the annual carol service at the parish church where all masters wore gowns and hoods. (I don't recall any head-dress.) My next encounter with academical dress was when I wore it myself in 1982 to graduate as a Bachelor of Science at Manchester. This was the first time that I saw doctors in full dress.

Only when I arrived in Cambridge later in 1982 did I begin to appreciate the full range of the subject—the windows of Ryder and Amies and of A. E. Clothier were great attractions and, from Ede & Ravenscroft, I bought a BA status gown. (Rather a poor quality item, I recall, in a soft material—second-hand, I'm sure.)

In the University Library, I discovered Statutes and Ordinances in the Reading Room and in particular the sections about academical dress—what it consisted of and when it was worn. Further, equivalent tomes from other universities were available on nearby shelves. In the larger bookcases at the north end of the Reading Room I discovered Shaw (1966), Smith and Sheard and, of course, Franklyn. Shaw had been published by Heffer's and I was able to obtain a copy of my own. (I presume I must have bought it from that establishment.) The next edition of Shaw was to appear in the windows of Ryder and Amies and I bought a copy of that immediately!

Meanwhile, I was discovering that, though one rarely saw the square cap in Cambridge, Statutes and Ordinances clearly indicated that it should be worn. I obtained one from Ede & Ravenscroft and wore it with gown when out of doors. I also realised that there were more occasions for wearing a gown than initially met the eye. One example particularly comes to mind. One day in the middle 1980s, I read a notice in the Cambridge University Reporter that the Chancellor (the Duke of Edinburgh) was to give a lecture on some ecological subject somewhere on the New Museums Site. Those wishing to attend could apply for a ticket. Either in the Reporter notice or on the ticket that I subsequently received (or perhaps both), it was stated that academical dress need not be worn. This immediately suggested to me that academical dress could be worn! I don't recall that any other member of the audience had followed the same line of thought, but I did receive a conspiratorial smile from a proctor (who, of course, was in academical dress).

On reaching the age of 24, I obtained MA status so bought an MA gown and removed the strings. In 1987, I bought PhD hood, festal gown and bonnet and used the first of these (with my existing gown and cap) when graduating in the Senate-House. The festal gown (in art silk and without lace on the sleeves of course—the only version then allowed) was late arriving, so Ede & Ravenscroft lent me one when I first needed one— a feast in Clare to which I was invited by the late Dr Gordon Wright (Senior Treasurer of Cambridge University Heraldic and Genealogical Society (C. U. H. & G. S.) since 1968).

In the very early 1990s, waiting outside Great St Mary's to go into the Senate-House for an honorary degree congregation (another occasion for wearing academical dress), a figure, whom I knew by sight but had never met, pointed out to his companion that here was a correctly dressed PhD in festal dress. I initiated conversation by saying that I had seen the figure's square cap graduate some time previously. This was my first meeting with Tim Milner—he had lent his cap to a fellow Petrean (known to me through C. U. H. & G. S.) for use in the Senate-House some weeks before.

At that time, Tim was very active in the Cambridge branch of the Cambridge Society. One day, probably in the early to middle 1990s, he gave a talk on academical dress to that branch in the University Centre (the 'Grad Pad'). Among other things, he referred to George Shaw's monograph on Cambridge dress and included a humorous reference to the text's confusion between 'yoke' and 'yolk'. After the talk had finished and the members of the audience were making their way out, an elderly bearded figure made his way to the front (where I was chatting to Tim) and said he was sorry that the speaker hadn't liked his monograph. This was George Shaw!

As Internet searches became possible, I put suitable terms into search engines to see what they might return. One day, such a search produced a reference to a monograph about the dress of the University of Hertfordshire. I contacted the author. I forget what I wrote, but I do recall that his reply included a query about how I had managed to come across his work. Of course, at that time, I had no idea with what a notable figure I had been corresponding!

In about 1996, an enquiry was sent around academic-related staff at Nottingham (where I had been since 1990) asking for stewards to help at graduation. I offered my services and, in my reply, I noted that I had an interest in academical dress. Not only were my services accepted but I was offered the role of Robing Room Steward. This entailed looking after the officers' robes and the gowns of the honorary graduates. It also meant I could renew my acquaintance with the then Esquire Bedell with whom I had done some computing a few years previously. When the then University Marshal retired a few years later, the Esquire Bedell was asked whether he could suggest any candidates for the now vacant position. He was generous enough to suggest me—the only occasion on which I have been headhunted!

At some time in the middle to late 1990s I had contacted George Shaw asking whether I could copy the Cambridge figures from his work and put them on the web-page of C. U. H. & G. S. as a guide for the society's members. Philip Goff spotted these pages and contacted me. We exchanged a few messages but before we could meet greater events intervened—the Burgon Society was being formed. I was invited to the second preliminary meeting (with Giles Brightwell, then at Sidney Sussex, playing some role in the invitation) at the University of London chaplaincy.

Following the second meeting, later in the day, Nicholas Groves wrote the following, rather conciliatory email to Br Michael who had been unable to attend.

```
Dear Michael,
I am sorry you couldn't be with us today; I hope your brother in religion has
  eased his way forth. This is in addition to the general posting I have just
  made. One of the topics that kept recurring today was that of the CIL, and
  its status - and its new sidekick, the ASL - (which is why I was chary of
  including it in a general posting!); people were very concerned that they
  would become the publicly accepted body dealing with acad. dress.
You may remember that at the last meeting, it was proposed that the e-group
  should become something more formal, but it was not seen as the right way
  forward. But in the light of today's discussions, we thought that a more
  formal group, looking especially into the history of dress, could usefully
be
  formed. So we are looking at setting up The Burgon Society, which will run
  alongside the e-group, and certainly not in competition! There has been, as
  I'm sure you will agree, a huge amount of very high quality research being
  done, and the feeling was that a formal group could usefully publish this
  more widely, and also affiliate to an umbrella organization, such as the
  Costume Society, and would also have more 'clout' when dealing with
  universities, Lambeth Palace and so forth (I would very much hope that
  meetings would be held in common - e.g. a trip to Lambeth to see the
  portraits and robe-cupboards!).
Obviously my reason for writing is that we do not want you to feel that we
are
  setting up a rival organization behind your back: it's more of a 'daughter'
  that has grown out of the original concept.
The exact form has yet to be worked out (we hope to have a meeting soon),
but
  will almost certainly involve electing members as Fellows (well, how could
we
  resist!), and very much hope that you will wish to be one of the first!
(FBS?
  FBurgSoc?)
All the best,
Nick.
==============================================
Nicholas Groves, MA
Lecturer in Early Mediæval Studies
nwgroves@ukgateway.net
```

To everyone's relief, Br Michael, replied to Nicholas Groves positively and here is an extract from his email:

```
>I am delighted that a more formal organisation should evolve from this
>group. I was a bit wary when we last met because we were few and there was
>no way of knowing how things would develop. Now that we have 60 members of
>the e-group, and it is clear that as well as being tat lovers we are also,
>and much more importantly, interested in an academic approach to academic
>dress, the setting up of a more formal organisation seems a very logical
>step, and one with which I would very much like to be associated. Another
>Fellowship - gosh! As long as there is no gingham involved .....
>It was considerate of you to contact me privately on this matter. Please be
>assured that rather than taking umbrage I am delighted at this new
>development. As I see you have copied your message to the "league of
>gentlemen" perhaps you would be kind enough to forward my response to them.
>Best wishes,
>Michael
>
>
>_____
>From Michael Powell, St Georges College, Weybridge, KT15 2QS, UK.
```

Two days later, on 19 June, Nicholas Groves had circulated the first draft of his original proposal for the Society's regulations, later renamed the Constitution, as seen in Figure 1.

The website

Meanwhile, Peter Durant had been giving much thought to a website for the Society and sent the following email:

Dear Fr. Phil

I haven't heard from anybody else apart from you.

I would like to act quite swiftly on the site and have something in place when the Society is launched.

What I was concerned about was not to be seen to be producing something without consulting anybody else.

On a purely practical level, you and I could decide on the contents, I could knock up a few screens and then we could invite comment from others. It would be easy to update the screens.

My initial ideas are as follows:

A Home Page with a welcome, possibly news items and/or details of any part of the site which has been updated; and obviously links to the other pages.

A page giving a brief history of Academical Dress. I thought perhaps we could use the text from the section in your London book, with scans of the pictures and diagrams, if you are happy with this.

A page giving a general schema for Academical Dress, i.e., who wears what. I have some ideas on this which I would like to talk to you about.

THE BURGON SOCIETY

draft regulations – for discussion
(those items enclosed in [square brackets] are suggestions to be finalized)

AIMS? (handwritten margin note)

demarkate some contrib. (handwritten margin note)

1. the name of the Society shall be THE BURGON SOCIETY, named after Dean Burgon, the only eponym of an item of academical dress – *viz* the burgon shape of hoods.

some interest (handwritten margin note)

2. the Society shall comprise (a) FELLOWS, who shall be engaged in active research into an aspect of the history of academical dress (b) MEMBERS, who are in sympathy with the aims of the Society, but not necessarily engaged in research. + ASSOCE

Members? by + of the history or design (handwritten margin note)

initially (handwritten margin note)

3. Fellows shall pay an annual subscription of [£10.00], for which they shall be entitled to receive all publications and other mailings of the Society, and to vote at meetings; Members shall pay a subscription of [£7.00], for which they shall be entitled to receive such mailings as the Council deems fit, and to attend meetings, but not to vote.

award? (handwritten margin note)

3a. Fellows may use the post-nominal designation [FBS/FBurgSoc/FBurgS], [and wear the Society's hood]; Members may do neither of these things.

ass to knowledge? (handwritten margin note)

4. Members may upgrade to Fellowship on the presentation of a paper at a meeting of the Society. — + more – *viz* by F'ship &

5. there shall be a Council of Management, which shall comprise [SIX] senior Fellows. Of these, one shall hold the post of Treasurer; one shall be Membership Secretary/Registrar; and one shall hold the post of Director of Research.

5a. the DIRECTOR OF RESEARCH shall co-ordinate the research, and keep in touch with Fellows on a regular basis. He shall keep records of ongoing research.

6. there shall also be a PRESIDENT, elected from the Fellowship, and who shall have a seat on the Council. *Unnecessary?*

7. a PATRON may be elected if so desired.

8. meetings shall be held from time to time, at which papers shall be presented for discussion. The public may be admitted. There shall be a General Meeting every year. Other meetings, in the form of outings, may be held as deemed desirable. Papers shall be published in an Annual.

9. the Society may affiliate itself to other organizations which promote the -historical study of costume.

10. a web-site shall be set up and maintained.

11. an archive shall be maintained, with especial reference to the past practices of / institutions, preserving the details of superseded or otherwise obsolete robes.

physical? (handwritten margin note)

12. it shall be proper for the Society to act in an advisory capacity to film and TV producers, or others who wish to ensure correctness in dress; also to those who wish to design robes themselves. NB: any Fellow is at liberty to act in a private advisory capacity, but must make it plain that he does not act in this case for the Society. It may also undertake commissions to design robes.

13. in the event of the Society being wound up, such monies as remain over shall be given to [*noble cause to be specified here!*]

14. this Constitution, having been once ratified at a General Meeting of the Society (for which [15] shall be deemed a quorum,) may only be altered by a further General Meeting called for that purpose.

Figure 1. First draft of regulations for the Burgon Society.

A page on the work of the Society with list of publications.

A page with an online application form.

A page of links to Statutes of Institutions (as on Dr. Horton's Site).

A page of links to Robe Makers.

An archive page with pictures or a list of items the Society holds (or will hold).

Tell me what you think. As for meeting, it looks as though I am free over the next few Saturdays. Evenings are also a possibility.

And in a later email Peter Durant wrote:

Also, I requested the www.burgon.org.uk web address on 20th June 2000, and it was secured on or before 22nd (i.e., 5 days after the June meeting) … .The website didn't actually go live until a few months later after I had built it and after we went public. I can't recall when that was exactly, but it was after the October meeting.[47]

Philip Lowe

Later in June 2000, I was contacted, at Ede & Ravenscroft, by Philip Lowe.[48] He had been investigating the various sets of robes made, over the years, for the Chancellor and Vice-Chancellor of Victoria University, Manchester, which, he believed, had been made by the company, although some of them bore the labels of another robemaker.

I invited him to visit me at the company's Chancery Lane premises where it quickly became apparent that he was another academic dress enthusiast. At the time he was engaged in writing up an account of Victoria University's academic and official dress.[49] I pointed him towards the Ede and Ravenscroft workbooks, archived in the Guildhall library and, later, he was able to find there descriptions and illustrations of the robes for which he was searching. He was also skilled in cutting and making academical and ecclesiastical robes and brought along some hoods to show me. Naturally, I told him about the plans for the Society and, as we shall see shortly, fol-

---

47 The Burgon Society website went live on 22 October 2000.

48 Philip Lowe, FBS, Foundation Fellow (and by examination); Member of Council (2000) first editor of Burgon Notes.

49 The Origins and Development of Academical Dress at the Victoria University of Manchester (privately printed, 2002).

lowing our meeting I wrote to him and we continued to communicate by email. Subsequently, he became a lively member of and contributor to the eGroup discussions and although work and distance prevented him from attending any of the meetings until the autumn, he quickly became part of our group.

Philip Lowe writes:

My teenage foray into academical and ecclesiastical dress occurred following the closure of the Methodist chapel I attended, and my relocation to an Anglican church similar in design to Gibberd's RC cathedral in Liverpool. Therein lay wonders of ceremonial such as processions and seasonally coloured eucharistic vestments. Equally intriguing was the odd hood-like black and silver appendage worn by the vicar over his full surplice at Evensong.[50] Soon many more were encountered at my grammar school, in multitudinous variety, on speech days, worn by masters with their gowns.

Serious (Saturday) perusal of University regulations at the local public library ensued: copying down (long-hand) descriptions of style, shape and colour, guided by G.W. Shaw's pioneering work and Hargreaves-Mawdsley too. Disbelief at one illustration (in 'Shaw') of a distinctive simple shape led to the receipt (gratis) of a Leicester Masters' hood and the first issue of 'Hoodata' from Messrs Ede & Ravenscroft ('We remain Master Philip your obedient servants … .')

Somewhere along the line occasional visits to Thomas Browns and Son, of Bridge Street Manchester, occurred where I acquired braid for making stoles and encountered the delightful manageress, Mrs Doris Palmer. This led to meeting the VC's Secretary for Ceremonials at Manchester, Miss Georgina Miller. I was put to task during the summer vacation doing repairs to a huge collection of scarlet and gold doctors' robes and hoods at the University, lunch being paid for out of petty cash as well as expenses for thread and bus journeys from Oldham. Thus connexions were established and a life-long interest nurtured.

Two decades later, in September 1999, I moved to work at the University Library. Realising that the archives from Owens College and the Victoria University were held on the premises, I saw an opportunity to investigate the history and background of the development of academic dress at Manchester, with its peculiarities, and which the dearth of records from Thomas Brown & Son had made

---

50 St Aidan's Theological College, Birkenhead, hood.

problematic. For my research I was trying to establish from whence had come the original c.1882 VC's and Chancellor's robes for the first Victoria University. I knew that a set from 1965/6, although it bore a Thos. Brown label had, in fact, been made by Ede & Ravenscroft, as had an older set from the 1930s. An advertisement in the University Calendar of 1883 led me to suspect that they had also made the original robes. Enquiries and phone conversations with Ede & Ravenscroft resulted in meeting Philip Goff at Chancery Lane, who pointed me towards the company's archive of workbooks held at the Guildhall, which confirmed my suspicion about the robes. Meanwhile, he had been discovering kindred spirits afflicted with the same fascination, and he explained that there were proposals afoot to establish a society. He thought that I would like to be involved and suggested a chat with Nick Groves.

Foundation Fellows

Between the second and third meetings there was much activity and our discussions took place on the academic dress Yahoo eGroup. It dawned upon us that if we were to be able to admit new fellows to the Society then we should need some pre-existing fellows in order to be able to do it. We therefore decided to regard the members of the eGroup as Foundation Fellows of the Burgon Society from 1 August that year, following the custom of the University of London, generally, to award its degrees on that date.

The eleven Foundation Fellows were: Giles Brightwell, Bruce Christianson, Matthew Duckett, Peter Durant, Philip Goff, Nicholas Groves, John Horton, Stephen James, Philip Lowe, Michael Powell and Robin Rees. The founders are represented in the Burgon Society logo, designed by Dr John Horton.[51] All but two of the founding fellows have remained as subscribing members of the Society, although, as I write,[52] and for the first time since its foundation, none of the founders is currently serving on the Executive Committee (Council).

Second Chaplaincy Meeting; inauguration of the Society

The inaugural meeting of the Burgon Society took place on 2 September 2000, again at the University of London Chaplaincy in Gor-

---

51 '[H]ence the eleven Andrewes caps flying around the Burgon hood on our logo', comment from Peter Durant, FBS, in an email to me of 25 April 2020.

52 December 2020.

LIST OF AGENDA

1. Introductions and Apologies for Absence.
2. Discussion of the Draft Regulations (led by Mr Nicholas Groves, MA, BMus, FSAScot.) – *already circulated; appended below*
3. Election/appointment of Officers: Treasurer; Membership Secretary; Director of Research; [Chairman]; [President]; Patron.
4. Honorary Fellows.
5. The Society Web-site (Mr Peter Durant, BA).
6. Publications.
7. Archives.
8. The Society Hood (see over).
9. Any other business.

*Fellows of the Society as at August 1ˢᵗ 2000, and entitled to attend and vote at the Inaugural Meeting (those marked * have tendered their apologies):*

Giles Brightwell, MA(*Dunelm:*), LTCL, FRSA
Bruce Christianson, MSc (*Victoria, Wellington*), DPhil(*Oxon:*), FNZMS
Matthew Duckett, BSc(*EAng*), MRSC, CChem, PGCE, FSAScot
Peter Durant, BA(*Econ*), PGCE
Philip Goff, BD(*Lond*)
Nicholas Groves, MA, BMus(*Wales*), MA(*EAng*), BA(*Lond*), PGCE, FSAScot
John Horton, BSc(*Manc:*), PhD(*Cantab:*), MInstP
*Stephen James, MA(*Reading*), EdD(*Bristol*), FTCL, FCollP, FRSA, MIMgt
*Philip Lowe, RMN, LTCL
*Michael Powell, MPhil, MEd(*Brunel*), ACP, MCollP, ACertCM
Robin Rees, BSc, MPhil(*Lond*), PhD(*Sefield:*), MAstatus (*Oxon*), CPhys, MInstP

Figure 2. Agenda of the 2 September 2000 meeting.

draft regulations – for discussion

SECOND RECENSION
   (those items enclosed in [*square brackets*] are suggestions to be finalized)

1. the name of the Society shall be THE BURGON SOCIETY, named after Dean Burgon, the only eponym of an item of academical dress – *vidz* the burgon shape of hoods.
2. the Society shall concern itself with the study of academic dress in all its aspects – design, practice, history.
3. the Society shall comprise (a) FELLOWS, who shall be engaged in active research into one of the above aspects of academical dress, or who have contributed significantly to one of the said aspects; (b) MEMBERS, who have demonstrated some contribution, but who are not necessarily engaged in research; (c) ASSOCIATES, who are in sympathy with the aims of the Society.
4. the Society may confer on persons who have made an outstanding contribution the distinction of HONORARY FELLOW.
5. Fellows shall pay an annual subscription of [£10.00], for which they shall be entitled to receive all publications and other mailings of the Society, and to vote at meetings; Members and Associates shall pay a subscription of [£7.00], for which they shall be entitled to receive such mailings as the Council deems fit, and to attend meetings, but not to vote.
6. Fellows may use the post-nominal designation [FBS/FBurgSoc/FBurgS], and wear the Society's hood; Members may use the designation [MBS/MBurgSoc/MBurgS], and wear the Society's hood; Associates....
7. Members may upgrade to Fellowship on the presentation of a paper on one of the aspects specified in §2 *supra*, at a meeting of Fellows of the Society specially called for that purpose; or by demonstrating a significant contribution. In either case, the application shall be subject to a vote of the Fellows present.
8. there shall be a Council of Management, which shall comprise [SIX] senior Fellows. Of these, one shall hold the post of Treasurer; one shall be Membership Secretary/Registrar; and one shall hold the post of Director of Research. There may be other posts created – e.g. an Excursions Secretary.
9. the DIRECTOR OF RESEARCH shall co-ordinate the research, and keep in touch with Fellows on a regular basis. He shall keep records of ongoing research.
10. there shall also be a PRESIDENT, elected from the Fellowship, and who shall have a seat on the Council.
11. a PATRON may be elected if so desired.
12. meetings shall be held from time to time, at which papers shall be presented for discussion. The public may be admitted. There shall be a General Meeting every year. Other meetings, in the form of outings, may be held as deemed desirable. Papers shall be published in an Annual.
13. the Society may affiliate itself to other organizations which promote the study of costume.
14. a web-site shall be set up and maintained.
15. an archive shall be maintained, with especial reference to the past practices of institutions, preserving the details of superseded or otherwise obsolete robes. This archive shall take the form of paper documents (including photographs and other pictorial representations) and actual items of dress. It shall be available for consultation by interested parties in such ways as the Society determines.

16. it shall be proper for the Society to act in an advisory capacity to film and TV producers, or others who wish to ensure correctness in dress; also to those who wish to design robes themselves. It may also undertake commissions to design robes. NB: any Fellow is at liberty to act in a private advisory capacity, but must make it plain that he does not act in this case for the Society.
17. in the event of the Society being wound up, such monies as remain over shall be given to [*noble cause to be specified here*]
18. this Constitution, having been once ratified at a General Meeting of the Society (for which [15] shall be deemed a quorum,] may only be altered by a further General Meeting called for that purpose.

nwg/19vi00/rev22vi00

SOCIETY HOOD

This is going to cause much discussion. Some basic questions to address are:

1. do we want one Society hood used by all (if so, who? i.e. do MBS and ABS get it as well) OR a different hood per membership grade (I would suggest here one for ABS and MBS, one for FBS and possibly one for HonFBS)
2. I would be anxious to avoid all these special 'foundation fellow' hoods and so forth which have proliferated in recent years; but we could consider special robes for officers – possibly a trimmed gown worn with the FBS hood.
3.

Some suggestions already received are (all burgon shape [s2], naturally...):
1. black lined ruby silk (as EdD etc of London); with scarlet lined ruby for special use.
2. a) dark red lined self, faced c5″ red & gold brocade.
   b) dark blue lined peacock faced c5″ blue brocade.

   c) black lined black faced c5″ purple & gold brocade.

3. black lined amaranth (as St Andrew's BSc).
4. amaranth lined black watered.
5. a colour lined grey fur for winter use and lined grey shot silk for summer use (reviving a medaeval custom).
6. deep red lined black & gold brocade.

Figure 3. Draft regulations, discussed 2 September 2000.

don Square. Eight members of the group were present: Giles Bright-well, Matthew Duckett; Peter Durant, Philip Goff, Nicholas Groves, John Horton, Stephen James, and Robin Rees.

Included with the agenda (see Fig. 2) was a revised version of the regulations for the Society, an update on the website and, of course, academic dress for the Fellows.[53]

---

53 Observant readers may have spotted a stain on the copy of this agenda scanned into this monograph.. Peter Durant recalls a prescient conversation about it: 'This was caused by [another of the members present] who tripped up spilling his coffee. I remember saying to him, "One day the spilling of your coffee will be captured in a painting depicting the formation of the Society" (or words to that effect).'

From: "Nicholas Groves" <nwgroves@ukgateway.net>
To: "philip lowe" <pjlowe@fs1.li.man.ac.uk>,
"Br. Michael" <BrMichael@St-Georges-College.co.uk>,
"robin rees" <robin.rees@oucs.ox.ac.uk>,
"bruce christianson" <b.christianson@herts.ac.uk>
Copies to: "Dr S N James" <snjames@email.msn.com>
Subject: burgons
Date sent: Sat, 2 Sep 2000 21:31:48 +0100

Dear All,

A very good and productive meeting, and we were all sorry you were unable to attend. Formal minutes will follow in due course, but the gist of the meeting was as follows (following my agenda paper): 1. apologies duly tendered! 2. the Regulations were passed in substance. A full revised text will follow, but the main points are: a] there will be Fellows and ordinary members. Anyone who is interested in the aims of the Society may be elected a member; to become a Fellow will involve reading a paper (c5000 wds) at a meeting, (or an equivalent series of short ones), or publishing either in the Society's Annual (or elsewhere) a 5000 wd article (or equivalent). It is accepted that many members will not wish to do this. In all cases, the Council shall meet to discuss the presented work, and vote on the outcome. Upgrade may also be by a significant academic contribution. b] Fellows may use the designation FBS and wear the hood; members may do neither. (cf Royal Hist Soc), nor may they vote at meetings. c] The Council. This shall comprise: Chair of Council; Membership Secretary; Registrar; Dir of Research; Editor; Communications Officer; up to 4 ordinary councillors, subject to re-election by the Fellowship. The posts of Webmaster and Archivist are filled as Council appointments, and are not subject to election by the Fellowship, and sit on the Council *ex officio*. In order to get things moving, we appointed today as follows, to be duly ratified; Chair: Phil Goff; M'ship:Matthew Duckett; Registrar: Stephen James; Dir of Research: Nick Groves; Webmaster: Peter Durant; Archivist: Giles Brightwell. John Horton is an Ordinary Councillor, and the names of the four of you have been placed there too for the time being. We would, however, be pleased if anyone would like to take on the empty posts: Treasurer, Communications and Editor. Any offers? (Communications would liase with universities, collections/museums and other tat societies, and act as press officer). d] we decided in due course to elect a President, this to be a ceremonial role like a Chancellor. Elected by the whole Fellowship for 5 years, with possibility of infinite renewals. e] A patron ditto, but probably several. f] The constitution will be ratified, and the procedure of AGMs will be drawn up by Matthew, and added to the end of the Articles already with you as para 19+ 4. Honorary Fellows will be created - a list of likely names is in hand. Any suggestions to Stephen (snjames@msn.com) asap, please. 5. You will have seen the website - if not, go here (while it's being revised): www.burgon.org.uk/prototype.html 6. Publications - we see as being the Annual/Proceedings, and the occasional monograph. 7. Archives - will be the Wardrobe and the Library. 8. The HOOD. Surprisingly little discussion. We were greatly impressed by Phil Lowe's 'specimen' hood, but the mind of the meeting was that the hood should be dark blue (Oxford/Oriel) lined with Oxon MA shot crimson - some debate still on whether the shell should be plain or brocade. Ceremonial robes for Council were adumbrated: Oxon doctors pattern, in dark blue with sleeves and facings of shot crimson, worn without the hood, but with the Bishop Andrewes cap (as Cantab DD) 9. AOB. ne Council meeting, for ratification of the constitution, on Saturday 21st October at 1100 am; venue probably in Senate House (Phil G to arrange) Please let Stephen have any comments on the above, Nick.

Figure 4. Report on inaugural meeting of the Society.

By the end of the meeting, the various officers of the Burgon Society had been appointed, namely: Chairman, Philip Goff; Registrar, Stephen James; Director of Research, Nicholas Groves; Membership Secretary, Matthew Duckett; Webmaster, Peter Durant; Archivist, Giles Brightwell. This left John Horton as an ordinary member of Council along with those unable to attend the meeting: Bruce Christianson, Philip Lowe and Michael Powell, and also the posts of Treasurer, Editor and Communications Officer yet to appoint.

Later that evening, Nicholas Groves sent an email to those who had been unable to attend, the meeting, giving a summary of the day's proceedings and also commenting on the Council's discussion of a hood for Fellows and robes for officers (see Fig. 4).

It can be seen from the note accompanying the agenda and Nicholas Groves's email report of the meeting (see Figs 3 & 4) that several suggestions for the hood were considered. At the outset there was a strong desire to use colours which had some connection with Dean Burgon's own associations with Oxford, particularly the dark blue of Oriel College together with the shot crimson MA silk lining; and some wondered whether the blue should be of plain silk or some brocade.[54]

Two days later, on 4 September 2000, following our meeting at Chancery Lane, I wrote to Philip Lowe and referred in my letter to the inaugural meeting of the Society (see Fig. 5).

The first Senate House meeting: Foundation Day

On Saturday 21 October 2000, nine of the Burgon Society founding fellows met in room 103 of Senate House, University of London. By then we had regulations (later the constitution), preparations for a website, the examining of candidates for the fellowship and a bank account. At the meeting, some of the other posts on Council were filled. We decided on 21 October as our foundation day and to hold the annual Burgon Society Congregation on the Saturday nearest to it.

Philip Lowe, who had by then finished his paper on the academical dress of Manchester Victoria University, as well as being counted among the founders, wished to be a fellow of the Society by examination and duly read in his paper at the meeting to unanimous

---

54 See also the section on the academic and official robes of the Society later in this article.

4·IX·00

Dear Phil,

Thank you for the Troods which I think are
very well made. Let me know if you
want some work. I return them herewith.

Here is all we have on the Manchester
Chancellor's robe. There is a reference no.
in the text and my colleague, Chris Allan,
is trying to follow it up.

We got much further with the Burgon soc.
on Saturday – Nick will bring you up
to speed.

Walsingham was very good, thank you,
but there seems to be so much to do
at present – I'm sure you know the
feeling!

Hope to see you 'ere long.

Yours sincerely,   Philip

Figure 5. Letter to Philip Lowe.

acclaim; the fellowship submission of Dr Noel Cox was read and approved, and he was admitted in absentia as a Fellow by examination.

Here are the minutes of that meeting of the Burgon Society at which names were proposed, and agreed, of those to be offered the fellowship of the Society, *honoris causa*.

The Burgon Society
Founded to promote the study of Academical Dress

Registrar: Dr S. N. James MA, EdD, FTCL, ARCM, CertEd, FRSA, FCollP, FBS, MIMgt

Minutes of the Meeting held on 21st October 2000

Present: Philip Goff, Nicholas Groves, Stephen James, Bruce Christianson, Matthew Duckett, John Horton, Peter Durant, Michael Powell, Philip Lowe.

Apologies: Giles Brightwell, Robin Rees.

Welcome: Philip Goff opened the meeting and conveyed welcomes from the Vice Chancellor and the Director of Administration of London University. Philip read a letter from Dr John Birch, who offered advice about the Society, including the proposed academical dress. It was agreed that the Registrar should reply to Dr Birch to thank him for his interest.

Ratification of the Regulations: The Final Recension (previously circulated), was discussed and various amendments and suggestions made.[55]

These included:

Confirmation that the name of the society shall be the Burgon Society not The Burgon Society;

The deletion of the reference in paragraph 1 to the only eponym of an item of academical dress, as there is a John Knox cap and a Bishop Andrewe's cap;

An enrolment fee of £20 to include the first year's membership;

An amendment in paragraph 8 to include a reference to the power of the Council to co-opt;

The deletion of the reference to specific amounts of money in paragraph 5;

The replacement of the word upgrade by the word proceed in paragraph 7;

Paragraphs 21 and 22 amended to include an entitlement to wear academical dress as prescribed;

The deletion of paragraphs 23 and 24;

It was agreed that Philip Goff and Nicholas Groves would confirm and circulate the final version.

---

55 The text of the regulations revised at the meeting on 21 October 2000 and adopted as the constitution appear at the end of the book.

Proposed Nicholas Groves, seconded Stephen James, agreed *nem. con.*

Ratification of the Officers:

Chairman – Philip Goff

Registrar – Stephen James

Membership Secretary – Matthew Duckett

Treasurer – Eoghain Murphy,[56] (subject to confirmation that he will have the time to undertake the duties)

Director of Research – Nicholas Groves

Archivist – Giles Brightwell

Webmaster – Peter Durant

Communications Officer – Philip Goff

Editor - Michael Powell

Ordinary Members of Council – John Horton, Robin Rees, Bruce Christianson, and Philip Lowe (subject to being elected a fellow—see Presentation of Research Paper below)

Proposed Bruce Christianson, seconded Michael Powell, agreed *nem. con.*

Website Update: Peter Durant gave a detailed update of the website. It should be ready to go live by the middle of next week. It was agreed not to have any password restricted sites. Philip Goff proposed a vote of thanks to Peter for all of his hard work and expertise in devising and maintaining the website. This was agreed *nem. con.*

Launch: In addition to the website, it was agreed to design and issue a leaflet in 1/3 A4 format. Peter Durant agreed to undertake the design. Once the leaflet has been printed it was also agreed to contact the ceremonial officers at each of the universities to make them aware of the existence of the society and to exchange information.

Proposals for Honorary fellowships: The following people were proposed:

Canon Harry Krauss, Hugh Smith, George Shaw, John Birch, Aileen Ribeiro, John Baker, Robin Richardson, John Venables, Graham Zellick, Kevin Sheard.

Proposed Nicholas Groves, seconded Bruce Christianson, agreed *nem. con.*

Date for Ceremonial Congregation: 20th October 2001.

Date of Next Meeting: 13th January 2001.

Any Other Business:

Academic Dress – This was discussed as part of the regulations.

Relationship with other academical dress societies – It was agreed

---

56 I have no idea what became of him and don't believe I ever met him.

that this should not be seen as a problem. As each society has different reasons for its existence. The Burgon Society will be seen as the society concerned with serious research and academic study of academical dress.

Society Tie: It was agreed to delay any decision until the membership had grown.

Presentation of Research Paper:

Philip Lowe gave a very interesting illustrated lecture based on his research of the Academical Dress of the University of Manchester. Following the presentation and questions, Council formally admitted Philip as a fellow.[57]

The next morning, Br Michael posted the following message on the eGroup site:

> As you may be aware, I founded this eGroup some two years ago in order to discover if there were any other people out there who shared my own interest in academic dress. At the time I thought I might find no more than a handful of kindred souls. I am delighted to find that the group now has a membership of more than 70 and a lively and fascinating volume of correspondence has ensued.
>
> Early on in the life of the eGroup a number of the more active members met in London, and at that time the possible establishment of a more formal grouping was mooted.
>
> Plans for such a grouping have progressed quietly over the months, and a great deal of hard work has been done by a number of people to put into place the foundations of a society whose aim would be the formal study of academic dress.
>
> As a result of all this planning and work, at a meeting held at the London University Senate House on Saturday 21st October, THE BURGON SOCIETY came into existence.
>
> I would, therefore, urge you to look at the Society's website which is at http://www.burgon.org.uk and consider whether you would like to put your interest in academic dress on a more formal basis by joining the Society. As the final details of the Society have only just been ratified the webmaster may need a day or two to update the site before making it fully available so please keep trying. It should certainly be available by Monday or Tuesday. I have put the address for the site into the 'Links' area of the eGroup.
>
> I would stress that the Burgon Society aims to become a recognised and respected learned society with a strong basis in formal research and study. With that in mind, I am aware that

---

57 And also Noel Cox, in absentia.

many eGroup members might wish simply to continue belonging to the rather more informal structure of an eGroup, and I would hope that our group will continue to provide a lively forum for the exchange of information about academic dress and related subjects.

I have accepted a position on the Council of the Burgon Society and I look forward to continuing to promote interest in academic dress with the Society and with this eGroup.

The three months from October until the next meeting were filled with activity as the minutes of 13 January 2001 show.

The Burgon Society
Minutes of the Council Meeting held on 13th January 2001
Present: Philip Goff, Nicholas Groves, Stephen James, Michael Powell, Peter Durant, Matthew Duckett.

Apologies: Bruce Christianson, Peter Lowe, Giles Brightwell, Robin Rees, John Horton.

Minutes of the Last Meeting: Agreed *nem. con*.

Matters Arising: None.

Membership Update:

I. Council were pleased to learn of the number of members who had enrolled since the last meeting.

2. It was agreed that members of the Council should pay the annual fee. Members of Council are requested to send cheques to Philip Goff.

It was noted that all the current membership are male. It was agreed not to introduce any form of positive discrimination.

4. Matthew Duckett highlighted the additional costs involved when dealing with overseas members. It was agreed to monitor the situation.

Proceedings/Journal/Transaction: The format for submission of research papers was discussed to ensure easy inclusion in an annual publication. It was agreed to authorise Nicholas Groves to amend the guidance for submission, to include instructions regarding format.

Website/Letterhead/Leaflet:

Website —

I. Various parts of the website have been updated including, the robemakers.

Various editions of Hoodata have been added to the website.

Peter Durant is keeping abreast of information in relation to search engines. He recommended that the Society join Search Engine Gold in the medium term.

Peter Durant presented statistics about the number of times the website has been visited.

Leaflet —

Peter Durant circulated a draft leaflet. Following some minor amendments, Philip Goff agreed to arrange printing (on cream matt paper).

Letterhead —

Peter Durant agreed to circulate a template, (via e-mail), to each of the officers.

Research Update:

I. Five people have enquired about fellowship since the last meeting. Of these, one has been approved and submitted his research paper, one has had his proposal approved and is currently working on his submission, one has had this proposal approved in principle and two have currently not submitted a proposal.

Following a successful submission, Noel Cox was formally elected a fellow. Proposed by Nicholas Groves seconded by Stephen James and agreed *nem. con*. Nicholas Groves will inform Noel Cox of his election.

It was agreed that a diploma would be produced possibly to include an embossed seal.

Diplomas will be presented at the first Congregation in October.

Treasurer/Bank Account: It was agreed to open an account with Natwest. The signatories to be Philip Goff, Matthew Duckett and Stephen James (any two of three).

Proposed Michael Powell, seconded Nicholas Groves, agreed *nem. con.*

Reply to CIL Offer of Hon CIL: It was agreed to decline the corporate offer from CIL but invite them to offer honorary awards on an individual basis to those they felt qualified. Michael Powell agreed to reply on behalf of the Council.

Election of President: Following a proposal by Philip Goff it was agreed to invite Dr John Birch to become the first Honorary President.

Proposed Philip Goff, seconded Stephen James, agreed *nem. con*. Stephen James agreed to write on behalf of the Society.

Election of Honorary fellows: It was agreed to invite the people nominated at the last meeting, to accept an honorary fellowship. Stephen James agreed to write on behalf of the Society. Members of the Council were invited to send Stephen the address of the people they proposed. They are: Harry Krauss (Giles Brightwell). Hugh Smith, Aileen Ribeiro, Graham Zellick, Kevin Sheard (Philip Goff). John Baker (John Horton). Stephen has the details for Robin Richardson and George Shaw.

Academical Dress: Philip Goff showed the meeting an example of a possible fellows' hood. This was Burgon shape, black corded silk, lined and bound shot ruby silk. It was agreed to adopt this as the official hood. Proposed

Michael Powell, seconded Nicholas Groves, agreed *nem. con*. Philip agreed to obtain a quote for producing the hood. Thanks were offered to Philip.

Any Other Business:

Nicholas Groves book on Lampeter Academical Dress will be launched on February 19th. Nick will circulate the details of how to purchase once known.

Ceremonial Congregation—Philip Goff will explore the possibility of using the Chancellor's Hall in Senate House, and it was agreed to invite Dr John Birch to be one of the speakers.

It was agreed to include Nicholas Groves' Discussion Paper No. I about standard terminology on the agenda for the next meeting.

Date of the Next Meeting:

12th May 2001 at 11.00 am at the University Chaplaincy, 48B Gordon Square, London.

The First President: Dr John Birch

Dr John Birch, organist emeritus of Chichester Cathedral, Custos of the Albert Hall organ, Professor at the Royal College of Music, and former President of the Royal College of Organists, and I had become acquainted in the late 1990s. He had been much involved in designs for the academic robes of the Royal College of Music (a Northam appointment) and had then turned his attention to the Royal College of Organists (an Ede & Ravenscroft appointment). In March 2000, as well as working together on designs for some new awards, we discussed how the wonderful triple-shot 'pearl' silk used in the robes of University of Wales music degrees since 1898, and in some of the RCO dress from 1971, had become by then (to quote him) 'a brown Crimplene sludge'[58] and we decided to remedy this situation. After several trials with a notable silk weaving company a satisfactory version of the original silk was decided upon.[59] This was fortuitous because some weeks later the University of Wales put its robing contract up for tender and the newly woven RCO silk was used in the robes of its music degrees and therefore the company was able to send a sample of the silk along with all the other beautiful shot silks of that University in the tender documents.

Being the holder of a Lambeth DMus degree, that had been awarded on Oxford dress, Dr Birch also complained about the poor brocade substitutes then being used for the robe and hood. With his encouragement, although it involved considerable expense, I

58 A modified Terylene fibre.
59 M. Perkins & Sons Ltd in Alton, Hampshire.

arranged for the cream figured silk damask with its apple blossom pattern to be rewoven by the same company.

I also used to meet Dr Birch at Lambeth Palace where he looked after the music for the degree ceremonies and I looked after robing at the ceremonies and the archive of robes. Naturally, we spoke much about the Burgon Society and he was interested in it from the beginning, writing letters of encouragement and suggesting ideas for its robes. Given his involvement with academic dress, he seemed an ideal person to be made a fellow, *honoris causa*, and also to be the first President of the Society and the members of Council agreed to this with gladness.

Dr Stephen James, the Registrar, wrote to him on 19 February 2001 to sound him out:

> Dear Dr Birch,
>
> Thank you very much for your reply to my previous letter, which I read to the Council at a recent meeting.
>
> At the same meeting the Council discussed the names of various people, including you, who might be prepared to accept an Honorary fellowship.[60] On behalf of the Council I am, therefore, writing formally to offer you the award.
>
> Those people who accept will be invited to attend a ceremony later in the year.[61]
>
> In addition, in recognition of your outstanding contribution to the subject, the Society would be honoured if you would also accept the invitation to be its first President.
>
> I hope you will feel able to accept both of these offers, and I look forward to receiving your reply.
>
> Yours, sincerely,

John Birch replied to this letter on 27 February 2001, as follows:

> Dear Dr James,
>
> Thank you so much for your kind letter, (which has been forwarded to me here in Cape Town) with its most interesting and flattering content. I shall indeed be delighted and honoured to accept an Honorary fellowship of the Burgon Society, and most happy to become its first President. The foundation of the Society is a most exciting, and I think much needed, concept; one in which I have had a considerable interest for more than half a century.

60 This should be fellowship, *honoris causa*.
61 The first Congregation, at Charterhouse on 20 October 2001.

I am replying to you by Fax, but I shall be back in Salisbury on Saturday, 3rd of March.

I see that you have, in the list of Officers, a vacancy for a Treasurer. I do know of someone who might well be a suitable candidate who has an interest I these matters. Perhaps you might like to meet him sometime in the future.[62]

With all good wishes to you and to the members of the Society, and with my gratitude to you all for giving me so much pleasure by your generous award of fellowship and by inviting me to be your President.

The first fellows *honoris causa*

Letters were received from others to whom the Registrar had written informing them of the Council's decision to offer them the fellowship of the Society, *honoris causa*. Space doesn't allow for all the gracious replies although there are letters of acceptance on file from Aileen Ribeiro, the only professor of a department of dress (the Courtauld Institute) in the country; Professor Sir John Baker, an authority of academic and legal dress; Professor Graham Zellick, the Vice-Chancellor of the University of London; Squadron Leader Alan Birt the founder and editor of Hoodata; Canon Harry Krauss of St Thomas', Fifth Avenue, New York, who had a long-time interest in the subject and, of course, Dr George Shaw. It goes without saying that we had also intended to offer the fellowship to Professor Hugh Smith but, very sadly, he died before the first congregation.

Delighted as we were with the acceptance of Council's offer of the FBS by such distinguished people, it was perhaps that of George Shaw that touched us the most. Following serious heart surgery, and increasingly frail, he gave the Society his imprimatur from the outset but before we could honour him in this small way he beat us to the punch by joining the Society and sending us a cheque for his membership, which was a little embarrassing. I hurriedly telephoned him to say that the Registrar was about to write to him to offer him the FBS. He was delighted by this.

Here is his acceptance letter of 25 February 2001.

Dear Dr James,

Thank you for your letter of the 19th Feb.

I feel greatly honoured to be invited to accept fellowship of the Burgon Society, and I have much pleasure in accepting.

---

62 See the entry on Ian Johnson.

It is my hope that the Society will be able to influence the present trend, which would appear to be shunning the use of academical dress, and also to correct some of the incongruities perpetuated by those who should know better.

With many thanks and best wishes.

Professor Graham Zellick, QC

At Ede & Ravenscroft, and based at the London office in Chancery Lane, one of my most important tasks was to look after the company's accounts and dealings with the University of London, both the central University and the colleges and institutes. As well as overseeing academic dress for the ceremonies, including Foundation Day, at Senate House and those held by the colleges, I also looked after academic dress enquiries on behalf of the university and eventually became responsible for assisting with the revision of the academical dress of the University in 1997. In addition, I submitted new dress designs for new degrees and diplomas and wrote-up the dress regulations which appear in the annexe to the University's Ordinances. This work brought me into contact with several vice-chancellors, as well as with principals, rectors and deans, some of whom, like the vice-chancellor of the University of London, Graham Zellick, took an interest in the robes of their institutions and with academic dress more generally. It was natural, therefore, that the Burgon Society should seek to have a distinguished vice-chancellor associated with it and he was made a Fellow of the Society, *honoris causa*, at the first Congregation held in 2001. Ten years later, he became a patron of the Society and since 2016 has been its President. In accepting the FBS, *honoris causa*, he wrote to the Registrar on 8 March 2001:

> Dear Dr James,
> I was delighted to receive your letter of February 28 and accept the offer of an Honorary fellowship of the Society with much pleasure.

The Patron

My own diocesan bishop, Dr Richard Chartres, was a well-known admirer of all things antiquarian and sartorial and that included academic costume. I wrote to him as follows:

THE BURGON SOCIETY
-for the study of academical dress-

Chairman of Council:
The Reverend Philip Goff BD AKC MBACP
24 Redhill Street Regent's Park London NW1 4DQ
020 7388 0580

The Right Revd and Rt Hon RJC Chartres DLitt DD FSA
The Old Deanery
Dean's Court
London EC4V 5AA

27th April 2001

You may recall me speaking to you about the Burgon Society and I am writing to ask you if you will do us the great honour of becoming our Patron.

I know that you have many calls upon your time and the cares of the Church and State weigh upon you. You are however a keen antiquarian and such interests provide some fun and relief in a stressful life as well as keeping alive the study of subjects regarded by most as trivial or outdated.

Since rediscovering my childhood hobby, some five years ago, I have found many people around the world with a similar interest in the funny bits of silk and fur with which human beings (primarily the British) mark their learning. On the Internet an initial group of those interested in the subject has grown into an international forum of 150 people of all ages and backgrounds. New members are joining us each week. The site may be found at: academic_dress@yahoo.com

The Burgon Society has grown out of this eGroup and is the more grown-up version of it. Several of our members are academics who have an interest in academical dress at a particular institution and are engaged in the task of keeping alive the history and traditions of academical dress within that particular university. Our web-site is at www.burgon.org do have a look at the site if you have the time.

Our aim is to connect with the major costume societies, dress departments of universities, museums, libraries and robemakers. Moreover we will encourage proper study of academical dress as a legitimate part of the study of costume as a whole. Legal and ecclesiastical dress, as far as it touches on academical dress, will also be examined.

We also examine for a Fellowship of the Society through our director of studies – a lecturer in medieval studies. Our first two such Fellowships have been awarded recently: one, just published, is for a history of academical dress at Lampeter before its incorporation into the University of Wales; and the other is for a dissertation on academical dress in New Zealand. Currently, work is being undertaken that will probably lead to published works on the academical dress of the universities of Manchester, Leeds, St Andrew's and Glasgow.

We will, in some way, be reviving the sort of study and writing encouraged by the Ecclesiological Society of St Paul. In this context we will be able to look at academic dress, as worn by the clergy, and examine how is has changed (deteriorated) or fallen into disuse. This may lead to some published work on clerical dress which might be of interest.

One of our first Hon Fellows will be Professor Aileen Ribeiro, Head of the department of dress at the Courtauld. She teaches an MA course in dress which can lead to the London MPhil/PhD. Past students of hers have written and published works on clerical and ceremonial costume.

Professor Graham Zellick is another recent Hon Fellow and well known to you.

Our President is Dr John Birch (past president of the RCO and RCM and former organist of Chichester and of the Temple). I imagine that you will remember him receiving the Lambeth DMus. I hope that the new Master of Charterhouse will also be associated with us. All three of us have various things to do with the Lambeth degree ceremony.

I think by now you will have caught the flavour of the Burgon Society. At present we meet at Senate House and we are evolving slowly so as to do things well and lay good foundations.

Please find enclosed a copy of our Constitution and Regulations.

It would be absolutely splendid if you were to associate your name with the Society and your patronage could be as active or inactive as your time allowed. Apart from the annual Congregation and business meetings I will probably organise the occasional meeting or dinner at the Athenaeum, for fun, with lively speaker.

He replied on 11 May, accepting this offer:

THE BISHOP OF LONDON

The Rev'd Philip Goff
Chairman
The Burgon Society
24 Redhill Street
Regent's Park
London NW1 4DQ

11ᵗʰ May 2001

Dear Philip

Many thanks for your letter and for the elegant enclosures explaining the purposes of the Burgon Society.

I am always vowing to reduce the number of societies of which I am a patron because I am always so ashamed of the very little time I can devote to their affairs. You have done me a great honour, however, in inviting me to be a patron of the Burgon Society and, casting good resolutions to the winds, I most gratefully accept.

With all good wishes and all success with the enterprise.

+Richard

The Rt. Rev'd and Rt. Hon. Richard Chartres DD FSA

THE OLD DEANERY, DEAN'S COURT, LONDON EC4V 5AA
TELEPHONE: 020 7248 6233 E-MAIL: bishop@londin.clara.co.uk FACSIMILE: 020 7248 9721

By this time, there was so much for us to do that we increased the frequency of Council meetings in the run-up to the AGM and Congregation of the Society, planned for the Autumn of 2001 and we assembled again on 12 May at Charterhouse.

The Burgon Society
Minutes of the Council Meeting held on 12th May 2001

Present: Philip Goff (Chairman); Nicholas Groves (Director of Research); Stephen James (Registrar); John Horton; Peter Durant (Web Master); Bruce Christianson.

Apologies: Michael Powell, Philip Lowe, Giles Brightwell, Robin Rees, Matthew Duckett.

Minutes of the Last Meeting: Amendment—Website-Search Engine Gold should be Web Position Gold. With this amendment the minutes were agreed *nem. con.* and signed.

Matters Arising: The Director of Research reported on the progress of the guidance for submission for research proposals.

Membership Update: Council was pleased to learn that six additional members had enrolled since the last meeting.

The Chairman proposed that an article be written to publicise the Society, possibly linked to the publication of Nicholas Grove's book, for submission to the THES, Church Times and similar publications.

Website/Letterhead/Leaflet:

Website—The Web Master reported the current position.

Various parts of the website have been updated including sections on research and a newsgroup.

A section is being developed to give links to various discussion topics.

The Web Master is keeping abreast of information in relation to search engines. It was agreed to authorise the Web Master to enrol the Society with Web Position Gold at a cost of €50 per annum, when he considered the time was right.

Statistics about the number of times the website has been visited were presented to the meeting. The most popular pages on the website, excluding the home page, are the society page and the wardrobe page.

It was agreed to publish the minutes of the Council meetings on the website, excluding any agreed confidential items.

It was agreed to add FBS to end of the list of qualifications for members of the Council, and to add FBS after the name of any fellow mentioned in any article on the website.

Leaflet—The Chairman circulated copies of the leaflet.

Research Update: The Director of Research reported on the responses to his request for thoughts about the inclusion of legal and ecclesiastical dress as research topics, which were equally divided for and against. Following a discussion, it was agreed to treat each proposal on its merits, but all research proposals must contain a link to academical dress.

Treasurer/Bank Account: The Chairman reported that a bank account has now been opened with the NatWest bank in Great Portland Street. Account Name: The Burgon Society, Account Number: [details redacted]. The signatories are Philip Goff, Matthew Duckett and Stephen James (any two of three). The Chairman will be pleased to receive cheques, (£20 payable to The Burgon Society), from any member who has not yet paid their annual subscription.

Election of President: The Registrar reported that John Birch had accepted the invitation to become the Society's first President.

Election of Honorary fellows: The Registrar reported that the following people had accepted the invitation to become Honorary fellows of the Society: Sqd Ldr Alan Birt (formerly Editor of Hoodata); Prof. John Baker QC, LLD, FBA (Professor at St Catherine's College, Cambridge); Professor Graham Zellick (Vice Chancellor of the University of London); Professor Aileen Ribeiro (Professor of the History of Dress at the Courtauld Institute, University of London); Dr John Birch (a past President of the Royal College of Music and Royal College of Organists and formerly Organist of Chichester Cathedral and the Temple Church); Dr George Shaw MA, MSc, D Phil, DSc, FIBiol (author of several books on academical dress); The Revd Canon Harry Krauss (Senior Curate St Thomas Church, Fifth Avenue, New York). Replies are awaited from Robin Richardson and John Venables. Members of the Council were invited to send the Registrar the addresses for Hugh Smith and Kevin Sheard, who still need to be contacted. It was agreed to include a list of fellows and Honorary fellows (*honoris causa*) on the website.

Patron: The Chairman reported that he had written to the Bishop of London, inviting him to become the Society's Patron, and was awaiting a reply.

Arrangements for a Ceremonial Congregation: It was agreed to postpone the ceremony until precise details had been agreed, including venue, robes, format, and availability of fellows, Hon fellows and guests. The Chairman agreed to contact the Vice Chancellor of London University to request permission to use of the Chancellor's Hall. The ceremony needs to be formal but not pompous. It was agreed that the majority of the next meeting should be devoted to this item.

Officers' Robes: It was agreed to keep to the pattern previously discussed and agreed. The Chairman highlighted the aspect of cost, although no decision was taken.

Annual: This should include extracts from research papers and other articles, and descriptions and photographs of the Society's robes.

Date of the Next Meeting: 14th July 2001 at 11.00 am. Venue to be announced.

Ian Johnson

The 'someone' to whom Dr Birch had alluded in his letter of 27 February was the indefatigable Ian Johnson,[63] who became the Treasurer and, additionally, the Membership Secretary, offices he has held, diligently, from very early days of the Society. Dr Birch wrote to me about him later in the year, on 12 July 2001. Here is part of the letter:

> Dear Philip,
>
> I would like to propose for the vacant position of Treasurer of the Society, Ian Johnson, BA, MCIM, AIL, M.Inst.D, FRSA, currently Treasurer of two charitable trusts: The Friends of Kensal Green Cemetery and The Mausoleum and Monuments Trust.
>
> He is most interested in the work of the Society and is extremely efficient (I think you met him recently at the Royal Albert Hall). I have known him well for over 25 years and I would think him an excellent addition to the Committee.

In the next meeting of Council, we appointed Ian Johnson formally as Treasurer and put together a timetable for the first Congregation of the Society to be held at Charterhouse the following October. Here are the minutes of the meeting:

> Minutes of the Council Meeting held on 14th July 2001.
>
> Present: Philip Goff (Chairman); Stephen James (Registrar); Peter Durant (Web Master); Michael Powell.
>
> Apologies: Bruce Christianson, Philip Lowe, Giles Brightwell, Robin Rees, Matthew Duckett, Nicholas Groves.
>
> Minutes of the Last Meeting: Amendment—Peter Lowe should read Philip Lowe. With this amendment the minutes were agreed *nem. con.* and signed.
>
> Matters Arising:
>
> Honorary fellows— 1. Robin Richardson had spoken to Philip Goff and John Venables has telephoned Stephen James, both supported the society, but had other time-consuming interests. Neither had formally replied to the offer of an Hon FBS. 2. The various categories of Honorary fellow, (e.g., *honoris causa* etc), were agreed. Peter agreed to update the details on the website.
>
> Patron—Philip Goff read a letter he had received from the Bishop

---

63 Ian Johnson, FBS, Member of Council and later the Executive Committee (2001–) Treasurer; Membership Secretary; Registrar and the prime mover in the work to see the Burgon Society through to its charitable status.

of London accepting the offer to become the Patron. It was agreed to offer him an Hon FBS. Stephen agreed to write.

Dress Regulations—The following amendment was agreed for the fellows' gown. The gown of the fellow's highest degree, or a black gown of the traditional Master's shape. Proposed Peter Durant, seconded Michael Powell, agreed *nem. con.*

Treasurer—Philip Goff read a letter from John Birch suggesting we approach Ian Johnson to be the Treasurer. Ian is the treasurer for several other organisations and is interested in our society. Philip has also met Ian. It was agreed to approach Ian. Proposed Michael Powell, seconded Stephen James, agreed *nem. con.* Philip agreed to contact Ian.

Website: Peter Durant gave an overview of the current position.

Arrangements and Date for Annual General Meeting: After much discussion it was agreed to combine the date of the AGM with a ceremony for the admission of fellows. The details were agreed:

Date—Saturday October 20th

Venue—Charterhouse—Philip Goff agreed to contact the Master James Thomson (who has offered us the use of Charterhouse for our meetings), to discuss suitable rooms and catering arrangements.

Times—

11:00 am—Meeting of Council to ensure all members are briefed and prepared for the AGM and ceremony. 12:00 noon—AGM to include the Chairman's report, a statement of the accounts and the election of officers.

12:30 pm—Lunch (for members of council, and not advertised).

2:00 pm—Ceremony for the admission of fellows. Stephen agreed to contact Nicholas Groves and jointly a suitable ceremony based on Nick's proposals.

Contents and Format for the Annual: The following was agreed:

Publish the annual at the AGM.

Format to be A3 folded with a glossy colour printed cover.

The body of the annual to be matt paper with black print.

Articles to include:

I.   A letter from the Patron.

A list of Officers and fellows, (including some pen portraits of the Honorary fellows).

The History of the Society.

Abstracts from Philip Goff's, Nick Grove's and Bruce Christianson's books.

An edited version of Philip Lowe's research.

Nick Grove's Discussion Paper No. 1.

A description (with colour plate), of the new Royal College of Organist's robes.

A request for scholarly articles for future annuals.

Membership Update: Council was pleased to learn that five members had enrolled since the last meeting.

Date of the Next Meeting: October 2001 at 11.00 am, at Charterhouse.

On behalf of the Council, I wrote to Ian Johnson on 28 July welcoming him to the Society, thanking him for agreeing to become Treasurer and informing him of the forthcoming Congregation on 20 October.

He replied on 7 August 2001 and was already on the case looking after membership fees and taking over responsibility for the bank account. He begins the letter by saying:

> Dear Philip,
>   Firstly, I have to say that I am delighted to be taking on the job of Treasurer. I look forward to working with you all in what seems a fascinating society.

Ian recalls those early events as follows:

I joined, or rather, was invited to join, the nascent Burgon Society in 2001. A close friend, Dr John Birch, had become President and as he knew I shared a distant interest in academic dress and the society needed a Treasurer he thought I might be interested in an involvement by taking on the job. It has to be said that my interest in academic dress was, more specifically, an interest in academic hoods. Like so many of my generation my interest in hoods was a result of attending a rather old fashioned grammar school. When I went up at 11 years old in 1963 a large number of the staff were Oxford or Cambridge graduates and the remainder from Durham, London, Leeds, Bristol and the RCA. Speech days were wonderful.

The job of Treasurer was not arduous in 2001 and over the next few years I took on a couple of tasks for the society including that of Registrar (as the secretary's job was known until the society became a registered charity in 2009). That post also included that of Membership Secretary.

I believe I am the longest serving member of the governing body of the Society.

The main project which fell to me to lead, other than managing the finances, was in 2008–09 when the society decided to apply for the status of a Registered Charity. As well as enhancing its status, Registered Charity status gives the Society greater ability to apply for funding and allows it to claim Gift Aid refunds on its subscriptions, again improving its finances. The main impediment to gaining the charity status was the fact that the society had decided at inception that it wanted, in order to maintain its academic research qualification, that only fellows would govern the Society. This was in conflict with the general rules of the Charity Commission. Happily our arguments were convincing and the Charity Commission accepted them in 2009. Since becoming a Registered Charity the Burgon Society has received around £7500 in Gift Aid.

Cyburcouncil[64]

As news of the Burgon Society began to spread, more and more of those who were interested in academical dress found and joined the Society and the Yahoo eGroup was busy with members exchanging information and discussing matters of interest. There was also much business to transact and the founders needed to keep in touch and make decisions between the meetings of Council. We therefore decided to have a separate internet forum in which we could get on with the business of the Society without intruding on the general discussions. At the Council meeting on 14 July, 2001, Br Michael was asked to create a new eGroup for this purpose:

> At today's Council meeting it was proposed that we should set up a private eGroup for the Burgon Society Council only so that we can discuss issues in private and if necessary have 'cyber meetings'.
> I have, therefore, set up an eGroup—or Yahoo group—called 'cyburcouncil'. You should all shortly receive from me an invitation to join. Please let me know if you don't.

Dr James Thomson

At Lambeth Palace, I also used to meet Dr James Thomson,[65] a surgeon who was chairman of the Lambeth Degree Holders Asso-

---

64 The initial members of Cyburcouncil were the eleven founders: Giles Brightwell, Bruce Christianson, Matthew Duckett, Peter Durant, Philip Goff, Nicholas Groves, John Horton, Stephen James, Philip Lowe, Michael Powell, and Robin Rees.

65 Dr Thomson, FBS, later became Vice-Patron, Patron and second President of the Burgon Society.

ciation, but I also knew him through visits, with my bishop, to his church in North London where he was an enthusiastic member of the serving team. He was interested in the Society and had recently become Master of Charterhouse, London. I therefore met him for lunch at my Club, following which, on 10th July, he wrote a very encouraging letter:

> Dear Philip,
>
> Thank you so much for a splendid lunch at the Athenaeum yesterday. It was so good to see you … .
>
> I was most interested in the Burgon Society and I was grateful to you for bringing my attention to it. What an achievement to establish this.
>
> I look forward to you coming here on Monday 10th September at 12.45
>
> Meanwhile I send warmest greetings and renewed thanks.

At the lunch, Dr Thomson had mentioned that it might be possible for us to hold some meetings at Charterhouse and therefore I wrote to him to ask if he would agree to host our first AGM and Congregation.

> It was very good to see you at lunch and thank you so much for your kind letter.
>
> Thank you also for the interest which you have shown in the Society, and I hope that, by now, you will have been able to visit our website at www.burgon.org.uk
>
> You were kind enough to say that, from time to time, we might be able to use Charterhouse as a place to meet. Is there a possibility that we could hold our AGM there on 20th October 2001 or another Saturday near to that time? Ideally, we should like to meet in the morning and then (in a very low-key ceremony) admit our fellows. If this second part to the proceedings were not possible at Charterhouse I would ask John Birch to find us a near-by church. As for refreshment, we would need to provide sandwiches over lunchtime for the AGM attendees and tea after the ceremony. This is something I can arrange or alternatively negotiate with you if you have the appropriate catering facilities. We should expect to pay for this, of course.
>
> At some point in the future we will have a formal Congregation but we have decided to begin cautiously and to take things step-by-step. We will not go for too much ceremonial early on and will worry about formal robes for officers later. However, we would expect to dress in our FBS hoods with the

black gown for anything ceremonial. Others attending would wear their own academical dress. I doubt whether we should get +Richard for October but I will ask him.

If all this seems too much there is a possibility of us going to Senate House since Graham Zellick, the VC, is one of our members. However, I hope you would still want to be associated with us.

I look forward to hearing from you and to seeing you in September.

Dr Alex Kerr

During this time, another academic dress enthusiast had found the Yahoo eGroup and members were already beginning to appreciate his knowledge and interest in the subject. Dr Alex Kerr[66] joined the Society in July 2001 and although he was unable to be present at the first Congregation, in October 2001, he has played a major part in the society from then on. He wrote:

Unlike others whose reminiscences figure in this account, I was not in at the beginning of the Society.

I first encountered academic gowns at Altrincham Grammar School for Boys, where I was a pupil from 1956 to 1964. Some of the masters wore their gowns in class and all of them did so for morning assembly. For speech day hoods were also worn and one chemistry master appeared in a Manchester (Victoria) doctoral full-dress robe. The School acquired two undergraduate gowns, which I now recognise as being in the Cambridge pensioner's [u1] pattern in one case and the Oxford scholar's [u2] in the other; they were worn in assembly by the head boy and the prefect reading the lesson. It was only much later, in 2003, that I learned George Shaw had been a pupil at AGS some fifteen years before me and was still in touch with a long-retired master I remembered too.

When I came to Oxford as an undergraduate in the mid-1960s academic dress was still in daily use for attending tutorials and some lectures as well as for formal hall, examinations and other formal events. I became fascinated by it and a fellow student

66 Dr Alex Kerr, FBS, Member of Council, then of the Executive Committee (2003–20) Publications Editor; Secretary; compiler of the Burgon Society online bibliography; member for the Editorial board for Transactions of the Burgon Society; examiner for the FBS.

gave me a copy of Shaw's 1966 book, which had been an unwanted present. I discovered several Ackermann engravings in Oxford print sellers' shops and started a collection.

When I graduated in 1967, being short of money I bought a second-hand BA gown and hood from G. E. Taylor at 19 Broad Street in Oxford, a one-man business with Mr Taylor running the shop himself. When I proceeded to the MA in 1971, I traded in my BA robes there for new MA ones. The shop closed in 1975, but I'm wearing the gown and hood, still in good shape, after nearly fifty years!

Finding that dealers in antique prints and staff in museums and libraries knew little about academic dress and cared even less, I had embarked on intermittent, lonely research. This included acquiring copies of Hargreaves-Mawdsley's book, Buxton and Gibson and various editions of Haycraft's catalogue—and later travelling to Camden Public Library to consult Smith and Sheard as there didn't seem to be a copy in Oxford then.

In 1979, I wrote to George Shaw to ask whether a new, expanded edition of his book or indeed a more general, popular book on academic dress had been considered. He replied: 'The idea of a new edition of Academical Dress has crossed my mind from time to time, but I fear that such a book would not sell. Only libraries would buy it ... and I'm sure no publisher would touch the idea.' He continued: 'The idea of a "popular" book on academical dress has been considered, but is of such limited interest, that I doubt if it would be taken up—if you know of any publisher who would be interested, I would be pleased to write such a tome! It's all a question of cash.'

In 1995, browsing in the Bodleian catalogue, I discovered that a book about the academic dress of the University of Hertfordshire had been published and wrote to the registrar to obtain a copy. My letter was passed to Bruce Christianson, the author, who was astonished that the title was already listed in the Bodleian and sent me a complimentary copy.

Like others who thought they were alone in their enthusiasm for the subject, I must have occasionally Googled 'academic dress' and was delighted in January 2001 to find that an online discussion and news group had been set up. I was not alone after all! I joined the group and in July that year joined the Burgon Society, looking forward to meeting like-minded enthusiasts, sharing discoveries and following up research on the history of academic dress.

Regretfully, in early September 2001, the Membership Secretary, Matthew Duckett, under pressure at work signalled that he needed to take a break. Events were moving fast in the Society and new people were joining all the time. We exchanged messages in the run-up to Congregation and the first Annual and, fortunately, Ian Johnson, the Treasurer offered to take on both roles.

On 18 October, 2001, as the day of the first Burgon Society Congregation approached I sent a message to colleagues on Cyburcouncil:

> Dear All,
>
> I went to a splendid solemn St Luke's Day Evensong at All Saints' Margaret Street, earlier tonight, in celebration of the centenary of St Luke's Hospital for the Clergy. It was arranged by James Thomson (Master of Charterhouse) who is also Vice-Chairman of St Luke's. He had persuaded all the medics present to wear their academic dress and a beautiful sight it was. I chaplained my bishop, who presided, and wore my Burgon hood, very proudly. Bishop Michael Marshall preached. Matthew (Duckett) was there as crucifer, it being his church.
>
> Also there was Sir Lionel Dakers (to whom I had mentioned the Society at a lunch for Lambeth degree holders a few weeks ago). He told me that he was so impressed (with BS) that he has changed his will and will leave all his robes to us. (James Thomson is also secretary of the Lambeth Degree Holders Association.)
>
> Anyhow, we had a chat about Saturday. We will arrive at 11 am, as arranged. It is probably best not to come earlier as you may be hanging around. I will come down with James at 10.45 or so, to greet people. We can then hold our informal Council meeting and also walk through the ceremony. Stephen has done the place names and has finished the programme (many thanks). Between our Council meeting and the AGM, Charterhouse will provide coffee and we can welcome anyone joining us for the AGM. For lunch there are many restaurants around Smithfield/Barbican/Farringdon ... We can then robe for the ceremony.

3

The First Congregation: 2001

The great day finally arrived and, thanks to the hospitable generosity of Dr James Thomson, the Master of Charterhouse and an early patron, the Burgon Society was able to have the grandest of beginnings in the grandest of settings, namely the Great Chamber at Charterhouse.

In the morning, the Council assembled at 11 a.m. for a brief meeting followed by the first annual meeting of the Society at noon (see Fig. 6), during which reports were duly received from the various Officers. I reported thus:

Chairman's Report
During the year there have been four meetings of the Council of the Burgon Society and one preliminary meeting.

Meetings of Council have taken place both at the University of London Chaplaincy, in Bloomsbury, and at Senate House.

Since our beginning we have set up the structures necessary for our society to grow and flourish: the Council itself; the Burgon Society website and our Internet forum, Cyburcouncil (should we use the correct spelling?), by means of which we conduct business in between council meetings and share information.

We have elected officers; designed a leaflet to advertise our aims and invite membership; and have generally set out our stall as a serious and learned society, keen to promote the study of academical dress, its origins, evolution, design and its place in the world today alongside other historic costume.

In order to further our aims, we have associated ourselves with eminent people, enthusiasts and specialists, as well as younger people whom we wish to encourage and who will, no doubt, one day replace us.[67]

We have in this first year ensured a good strong foundation on which

---

67 A prescient remark although inevitable!

Figure 6. Council meeting on the morning of the first Congregation at Charterhouse from (clockwise from centre foreground) Les Robarts (a fellow attending the meeting but not a member of Council), Nicholas Groves, John Horton, Bruce Christianson, Philip Goff, Stephen James, John Birch, Ian Johnson.

to build for the future. Unlike the temperamental Dean from whom we take our name, we have worked together with common goals in a fraternal spirit.

During the year our Director of Research, Nicholas Groves, saw his work on Lampeter published and we remain hopeful that Philip Lowe's study of academical dress at Victoria University, Manchester will also be published.

I shall have more to say, by way of thanks, in my words during the ceremony. For now I should like to hand over to Ian Johnson who will present the report on membership and finances.

Reports followed from the Director of Research and the Webmaster.

Those being admitted as fellows and their guests began to arrive and 2 p.m. we prepared to enter the chamber for the ceremony to install the President and to admit fellows. The first ceremony itself was (as it continues to be) rather solemn, but soon gave way to refreshments and the opportunity for much warm meeting-up and exchange of news.

The Patron, the Bishop of London, sent the following message to be read to the assembly:

Fig. 7. Dr John Birch, having been installed as President, admits Dr George Shaw to fellowship.

It is my great pleasure to greet the first Congregation of the Burgon Society. As your Patron, I wish the Society success in maintaining ancient traditions and in communicating the way in which academic dress represents a visible symbol of hard-won achievement on the part of graduates.
+Richard Londin.

A press release at the time records the activities of the day and the extraordinary collection of distinguished people who were, by then, associated with the Society. It was also published in the first *Burgon Society Annual* and reads as follows:

On Saturday, 20 October, the first Congregation of the Burgon Society was held at Charterhouse in London. Two fellows by submission were admitted: Mr Philip Lowe, a Foundation Fellow, for his work on the history of the robes of Manchester University, which we very much hope will be published in the near future; and Dr Noel Cox, for his work on the robes of the universities of New Zealand which he has generously published on the Internet.

Mr Ian Johnson, our Treasurer and Membership Secretary was admitted to fellowship of the Society *de jure*.

Also admitted as fellows *honoris causa* were: Dr George Shaw, author of several works on academical dress (see Figs 7

Fig. 8 The Chairman, the Revd Philip Goff, and Dr George Shaw, a new Fellow, admire Dr Charles Franklyn's illicit University of Lausanne doctoral habit after the first Congregation as other Fellows and guests watch.

and 8). Professor Graham Zellick, QC, Vice-Chancellor of the University of London; Professor Aileen Ribeiro, Professor of the History of Dress at the Courtauld Institute of Art; Squadron Leader Alan Birt, a long-time enthusiast of academical dress and author of 'Hoodata'; Professor John Baker QC, Professor of Law in the University of Cambridge, and author of several learned articles on the subject and the Revd Canon Harry Krauss, Senior Curate of St Thomas's Church, Fifth Avenue, New York, and President of the Board of the College of Arms Foundation, London.

The Society's first President, Dr John Birch, was installed, and a message from the Patron, the Bishop of London, was re-read. After the ceremony, in the Great Chamber, the Master, Dr James Thomson MS, FRCS, gave a talk on the history of Charterhouse and led fellows and guests on a tour of the buildings.

The Annual & Transactions

As set out in the constitution the Society began to produce a yearly record of its proceedings together with scholarly articles about academic dress. For a few years it was known as the *Burgon Society Annual*, but soon became a much more professional journal called *Transactions of the Burgon Society*, thanks to the skills of Dr Alex Kerr.[68] The first edition included, amongst other things, Nicholas Groves's article: 'Towards a Standard Terminology for describing Academic Dress', which was another milestone in the story of the Society and has provided a common language for academic dress researchers and enthusiasts to use when speaking or writing about the costumes.[69]

Following the Congregation, Dr Birch, the newly installed President, wrote in his inimitable style, sending congratulations on the success of the occasion but, as always, given his eagle-eye for detail, he includes one or two caveats, proving again, as if any of us had any doubts, what a good choice he had been for that office. (See Fig. 9.)

I was also delighted to receive a letter from Br Michael, the founder of the original eGroup, through which so many of us had met and had then decided to form the Society. Part of it is reproduced below:

JOSEPHITE COMMUNITY

St George's College
Weybridge Road
Addlestone
Surrey KT15 2QS
Tel: 01932 830457 / 830444
Mobile: 07720 706855
Fax: 01932 842268
Email: brmichaelpost-georges-college.co.uk

From the Community Bursar
Brother Michael Powell CJ

20th October 2001

Dear Phil,

Thanks very much for organising today. I thought it was a splendid occasion which set just the right tone for the Society: formal and sincere, yet without pomposity. I also thought that the setting was exceptional and that the Master was a wonderful host.

---

68 And, of course, in its present form, those of Professor Stephen Wolgast.

69 At <https://newprairiepress.org/burgonsociety/vol1/iss1/>.

Dr John Birch Fielding House The Close Salisbury Wiltshire SP1 2EB
Tel: (01722) 412458. Fax: (01722) 412368

22 October, 2001

The Reverend Philip Goff, BD, AKC, FBS,
24, Redhill Street,
Regent's Park
LONDON NW1 4DQ.

Dear Philip,

My warmest congratulations to you on the day at Charterhouse. Your organisation of the whole event was immaculate, and everything ran very much according to plan. I do hope that you were pleased. As I think I mentioned to you before we left, James Thomson said that we were always welcome to return, and I wonder, if your committee is agreeable, whether we ought not to confirm this, together with an appropriate date as soon as possible.

All my reactions were highly favourable, except for a few points.

I think a procession is as impressive in silence as it is with music. I personally found the musical interlude tedious in this particular ceremony and I couldn't quite divine its purpose; furthermore, the work chosen more than rather too long. It was masterly the way you weighed in with your applause to stem any further movements. (I am not commenting on the performance-simply the place of music.)

Putting hoods on from the front is difficult, though, no doubt with a little practice one may become more efficient at it, and I wonder if the Lambeth procedure is not better suited. Perhaps next time, the honorees ought to be made to replace their mortarboards, so that the doffing can be achieved after the conferment!!!

It is a matter of interest that one of the Brothers should have joined the Society, and I imagine that this will make a worthy entry in the journal. Also there was a membership form returned from Roger Greenacre, which will bring the membership to 47. Unfortunately Ian made a slip in his mathematics, corrected by our Swedish member, and for 55 it should read 45, and this ought to be corrected in the minutes.

The Burgon Society, being an arbiter for taste and for standard, I think that in the future a line ought to be taken between 'kosher' and 'non-kosher'!!!! This is perhaps something that initially we should discuss privately between ourselves, but, there may be, from time to time, various diplomas that we choose, in our wisdom and experience, not to recognise, lest, by so doing, we cheapen our own value and credibility. I suspect that in this matter we are probably 'singing from the same hymn sheet', nonetheless, I would hope that we can distance ourselves from non-academic self-congratulatory bodies. I think that in our early days we still have a tightrope to walk until our standards and principles are generally recognised, and I would hope that we can start year two in the way that we intend to continue.

I imagine that, if we stay at Charterhouse, there will not be a guided tour each year. Perhaps, if it is thought agreeable, the brothers might be invited to join us for tea if they so wish. It would give them someone new to talk to! This depends on how much you think we ought to cement our relationship.

I much enjoyed meeting the council in the relatively short time available, and look forward to the next occasion when I can get a better picture of who's who.'

Let us meet soon.

Renewed congratulations and my sincere thanks for giving me so much pleasure by making me your President.

Yours ever.

John

Fig. 9. Letter from Dr John Birch after first Congregation.

And a letter from the Treasurer, Ian Johnson:

21 October 2001

Dear Philip,

A brief personal note to thank you for the kind words and warm welcome yesterday. I am also very appreciative of the gift of the hood.

I enjoyed the day very much. I have to confess that I was quite apprehensive but my fears were quite unwarranted. The Society seems be a wonderfully pragmatic and friendly group of people.

I look forward to being part of it.

Kind regards

Sincerely

Ian.

Taking stock

By the time of the first Congregation of the Society, we had added or attracted to our membership a group of people with a wide range of expertise in our field, including authors and academics as well as those who were pursuing the fellowship by examination. We were also becoming known in other parts of the world from Europe to the US, Hong Kong, Thailand and New Zealand.

Later in the week, after the Congregation, on 25 October, I posted a message on the Cyburcouncil site by way of some Burgon Society housekeeping:

> Dear All,
>
> Thank you to Nick and Bruce for the Congregation report. Stephen and Giles, could you fill in the missing stuff on our fellows hon. causa please?
>
> Thanks, Peter, for updating the website. What about my other suggestions as to the list of Officers?
>
> I agree with Ian that we need to look serious by charging a sensible annual subscription – we also need to build up some money in the bank.

Michael has said that he will do his best to get the annual out before Christmas. Please let us know how you are getting on and whether you need more material or some help.

Phil L(owe), do you think you could do another version of the Burgon Congregation advert—a sort of general one that we can try in various journals like the church music ones, Times Higher etc? Just a thought. Others might also like to do this.

I had a very good email chat with Dr Alex Kerr. We hadn't missed him out and he didn't attend any of the initial meetings. However, he is very keen on joining us[70] and has, apparently, been in touch with Nick about the FBS by submission. I believe he is interested in a.d. in portraiture, which is a study sorely in need of being done.

I thanked everyone for their contribution to making the Congregation a success and apologized for omitting to thank Dr John Horton, the Marshal:

> ... could I put that right by saying what a splendid and professional Marshal we had! Have you (John) had more thoughts about a hat? A really old-fashioned silk velvet Tudor bonnet would look great with your gimp and velvet robe but you may have other ideas.

Increasing the membership

It did not go unnoticed, however, that interest in our particular branch of dress was overwhelmingly male whereas most costume societies are overwhelmingly female in their following and it was something of a relief when we were joined by Kerstin Fröberg, an independent robemaker in Sweden.

Kerstin Fröberg

It was the 13th December 1998. I was on a ladder painting a wall, when the 'phone rang. It was the (soon-to-be) pro-vice chancellor of the (soon-to-be) University of Växjö, who asked me if I wanted to make some 'coats' for the new professors who were to be installed in February. (He knew of me as 'a textile person', but we had never met.) Could I come in to discuss the idea?

Of course, I went and met with him and the vice-chancellor (whom I had met before). They needed some 'coats' to use on the 9th February, because there were several of the professors who were foreigners, and 'it might look like a circus' if they were to use what they wanted.

---

70 On the Burgon Society Council.

I have described some of the process earlier so I will leave that out.[71] In essence, it was an ... interesting ... process, both for designing and for logistics (where does one find some 120 metres of fabric, any fabric, rather before Christmas than later?), but on the 8th February I delivered 14 robes of a horrible design.

Of course, I knew nothing about AD—it is not much used in Sweden. Of course, I Googled it (or was it Alta Vista at that time?), and of course I did not find much. I knew that the Chaplain of Växjö cathedral was British, so I located him. He kindly showed me the robes of the Cathedral but could not help me further ('I wore one but did not really pay attention').

By then I decided that I had to get at least some basic knowledge, so when I visited my brother-in-law near Cambridge later that spring, I asked his help. We went to Ryder & Amies where I found Shaw I.

I continued searching the 'net, and at some point I found the Yahoo group.

Susan North

At the first Congregation we had admitted to fellowship (in absentia), Dr Aileen Ribeiro, of the Courtauld Institute, the only professor of a department of dress in the country. Through her, I had been put in touch with one her former MA students, Susan North who, by then, was curator of fashion and dress at the Victoria and Albert Museum. I wrote to her a few days after the Congregation to tell her about the Society.[72] She replied:

> Dear Philip,
>   Thank, you so much for your message and the details about the Burgon Society. What a wonderful website! If you like, I would be happy to pass on the details to costumes societies here and in North America, if you haven't already done so. It's the type of information they are keen to pass on to their members.
>   Is it possible for me to become a member of the Burgon Society (only a very humble, ordinary one, as I have no experience in the subject)? I'm so pleased to see what progress you have made with academic dress.

---

71 'Through the Needle's Eye; or, How I Became a Robemaker', Kerstin Froberg, FBS,*Transactions of the Burgon Society*, 11 (2011), pp. 6–7.

72 Dr Susan North, FBS, Member of Council; Communications Officer; Archivist.

Replying to an email I sent to her on 15 May 2020, Susan wrote:

> ... Has it been 20 years since Burgon began?? How quickly the time has flown ... . And how did I get involved? I'm sure that you contacted me first and I'm fairly certain that it must have been via Aileen (Ribeiro). I was one of her students at the Courtauld Institute on the History of Dress MA and we had a lecture on legal dress (with mention to its connections to AD). Why did I join? I'm a dress historian and curator of a dress collection. I'm interested because it is relevant to the historical periods I cover at the V&A. (My title as 'curator of fashion', is too limiting; I consider myself a social historian who happens to focus on dress and so include all aspects of clothing.)
>
> Early days? There was the exhilaration of inventing ourselves—deciding and defining what we were going to do in terms of activities and publications and the Burgon collection is unique, although keeping ourselves going is no less interesting.

The Spirit of the Founders

From the first Congregation onward, the Society grew rapidly, attracting new members and candidates for the fellowship; making itself known, for example, by writing to all the university registrars in the UK, and making contact with authors and experts in the field in other countries. Internet pages on the subject of academic dress increased very quickly along with references to the Society and offers came in from those who wished to donate robes. It was a very busy time for the Council members but there was a real sense of us being engaged together in something quite special, the scale of which none of us had quite foreseen.

There is so much more that might be written about the early years of the Society and future editions of TBS might continue to chronicle the story but this article is about how it all began. Although it has been rather long, I hope it has captured some of the enthusiasm, fun and excitement which we founders both experienced and intended for the Society along with our insistence that this should be underpinned by serious academic research. The social philosopher Eric Hoffer famously said that 'every great cause begins as a movement, becomes a business, and turns into a racket.' Whilst I don't, for a moment, think that this has happened to the Burgon Society, it is in the nature of successful organizations that they become more institutionalised as they put in place the necessary structures of gov-

Fig. 10. *President and nine of the eleven founders at the first Congregation. Back, left to right: Philip Lowe, Professor Bruce Christianson, Nicholas Groves, Dr John Horton, Peter Durant, Dr Robin Rees, Ian Johnson, Br Michael Powell. Front, Prof. Graham Zellick, Fr Philip Goff, Dr John Birch, Dr George Shaw, Dr Stephen James.*

Fig. 11. *Dr John Birch, Dr John Horton, Professor Bruce Christianson, Fr Philip Goff, and Nicholas Groves.*

ernance required to allow them to operate efficiently and smoothly on a larger scale. Those of us who founded the Burgon Society are delighted to see it grow and prosper but, even more importantly, are very keen to see the Society continue to promote the enthusiasm, fun and excitement which first inspired us and led us to the Society's foundation.

Nicholas Groves, in his brief first history of the Society, published in the *Burgon Society Annual 2001*, provides a fitting summary of those early years.

A Short History of the Burgon Society
Nicholas Groves, MA, BMus, FBS, FSAScot (Director of Research)

The Burgon Society has been in existence for a little over a year—we take 21st October 2000 as Foundation Day—and so this will be a very short history!

The origins of the Society lie in a web-based discussion group founded by Michael Powell on July 10th 1999. Initially, there was little activity, until it was discovered by Philip Goff (now Chairman of Council). He sent invitations to join to various other people he knew who had a similar interest, including myself, and it gradually gained members. (The current membership stands at 221; the address is http://groups.yahoo.com/academic_dress.)

An informal meeting of members was held in The Wheatsheaf Inn in Rathbone Place on 13th November 1999, and two further meetings followed on 17th June and 2nd September 2000, both at the University of London Chaplaincy, Gordon Square. From the very first, a desire was expressed to complement the e-group with a more formal society, which would undertake to promote research into the topic, and to publish it in a more permanent form. Out of the third meeting the Society was born, and the inaugural meeting of Council was held in the University of London Senate House on 21st October 2000 (which by a happy chance is the day in 1841 when Dean Burgon matriculated as an undergraduate at Worcester College, Oxford). It is good that the Council represents, in terms of the universities from which its members graduated (and in many cases, work) the entire spectrum from Oxford and Cambridge, through the 19th century federals (London, Wales, Victoria) and the redbricks (e.g. Exeter, Bristol) to the 1960s foundations (e.g. East Anglia, Brunel) and the re-designated polytechnics (e.g. Hertfordshire).

It was determined from the beginning that, while maintaining an open membership policy, there would be an examination available to those who wished, leading to fellowship of the Society (FBS). In order to make it as flexible as possible, the examination was laid down as being a substantial essay (or an equivalent number of shorter ones) on an approved topic, either published already or specially written; published is interpreted to include web-published work. Whenever possible, new fellows are invited to read their work before the Society as a form of formal examination. As the fellowship is examined, and as the Society deals with academic dress, it was felt right that a hood should be designed for fellows. Many and varied designs were submitted and considered, but the final design won unanimous approval as being both distinctive and restrained.

Once the Society was on a secure basis, we were able to invite other people well-known in academic dress circles to become honorary fellows—all of whom accepted; and we were also delighted to be able to secure Dr John Birch as President and the Bishop of London as Patron. At the time of writing, membership stands at 54 with 2 fellows by submission.

So why the Burgon Society? Several years ago, I had tried to get a similar society off the ground, but without any success. It seemed right that it should be named after the only person who had designed and become the eponym for an article of academic dress (the John Knox cap seems to have been named for him because he wore it, but did not design it). The Very Revd John William Burgon (1813–88) spent much of his life in Oxford, where he matriculated at Worcester College in 1841, and became a fellow of Oriel College in 1846. He held a number of curacies between 1849 and 1863, when he returned to Oxford to become vicar of St Mary-the-Virgin, the University Church. He held this post until 1876, when he became Dean of Chiches-

Dean John William Burgon

ter, where he remained until his death. As is known to those who study academic dress, the Oxford MA and BA (and indeed hoods for other degrees) may be made in one of two shapes—the 'plain Oxford' [s1] and the Burgon [s2]. This latter is a fuller cut and allows more of the lining to be turned and seen. One theory we have heard is that it was introduced to stop the robemakers skimping on the fur lining of the BA hood! It is still unclear exactly what the connexion is between the Dean and the hood pattern, and this is a topic of research we intend to pursue.

It is from Dean Burgon's two colleges that we take our colours—the corporate colours of blue, crimson, and white are from the Oriel colours of dark blue and silver, with the crimson of the Oxford MA hood lining added; the FBS hood, of black lined shot pink, comes from the Worcester colours of black and pink.

This is a short history, chronicling a short time, but I hope it will save a future historian of the Society a great deal of effort!

4

The Robes of the Burgon Society

It would have been most odd if the Burgon Society, whose strap line is 'for the study of academical dress', had not given thought, in the course of its proceedings, to some dress of its own. In fact, a lot of discussion took place on this subject from the very earliest meetings and, in some ways, this was the light-hearted counterfoil to a lot of hard work and planning for the formal society and also fulfilled our original two-pronged resolve: to enjoy our hobby as well as to further and disseminate knowledge about this branch of both historic and contemporary costume. Discussion about academic dress had, of course, preceded the notion of a formal body and members brought along some of their favourite or most interesting hoods to early meetings which, as I recall were full of laughter as we competed in our suggestions for the most glamorous and sometimes outrageous hoods. At the very first meeting, and solely for fun, one member brought a hood lined with pink-checked Gingham for our inspection.[73]

The discussion about the FBS hood continued online as Nicholas Groves reminded me of an example:

> I have now found a note that the purple-and-cream and cream-and-rose hoods were Michael's suggestions. From his e-mail to me 23 June 2000:
> We need to be aware that many of the people who will be interested will have several hoods already, so the colour scheme needs to be slightly out of the ordinary. I remembered that in my early days of 'tat lust', I used to read through Haycraft and pick out the hoods that I felt had a 'wow' factor, many of which were in the Asian section. I realise that the colours listed are

---

73 This had been presented to Giles Brightwell by colleagues at Sidney Sussex College, Cambridge.

already taken, but some of the institutions may have gone, or no longer award European academic dress, but here is one that I really like and may form a basis for discussion:

Mid-purple lined and bound cream (BScEng Benares).

I think cream is rather elegant and it is not very usual. Other colours which are not 'run of the mill' and could be quite elegant are rose and yellow (not necessarily together!) Maybe even white as a body colour.

(There is then an attachment with sketches of the two hoods).

Naturally, once we had decided to go ahead with forming the Society everyone was keen to contribute to the debate about its robes. Discussion about the FBS gown and hood and officers' robes took place at the inaugural meeting of the Burgon Society (the third meeting of the founders, and the second at the Chaplaincy) on 2 September 2000. As might be expected for such a society there was no shortage of ideas! The Registrar, Dr Stephen James, collected together many of the suggestions for the hood to present to the meeting. Fortuitously, at that meeting, Nicholas Groves made some notes about who had possibly suggested which hoods and he was able to send me a copy:

- black lined amaranth
- amaranth lined black
- amaranth lined grey fur (winter) or grey shot silk (summer) - *I have a feeling these three were Bruce's idea*
- navy damask lined and bound cream (the colours of Oriel College) - *no idea whose this was*
- red lined black and gold damask - *this may have been Phil Lowe also - see below*
- black lined ruby shot - *I think Phil Goff's suggestion*
- palatinate purple lined white damask - *possibly Giles' suggestion*
- black damask lined pearl shot - *might have been my idea*
- grey lined scarlet - *noted to be based on the Chichester canons' almuce/tippet, so maybe Dr Birch*

These I know were Phil Lowe's idea, and he
made examples some up:

- dark red lined crimson, bordered 5" red/
gold Fairford
- dark blue lined peacock, bordered 5" blue
Fairford
- black lined black bordered 5" purple/gold
Fairford

And a note that we'd had one request to avoid
the use of fur.
An MS note says 'black lined black watered'.

'Dignified and beautiful'[74]

We considered whether to have robes for our members as well as
for fellows,[75] but agreed that we didn't want to emulate those societies (which are legion) for which one simply pays a subscription and
then receives, in turn, the right to wear robes (the designs of some
of which seem to change frequently and become ever more exotic).
We intended no slight or judgement upon societies which did this; it
was simply a matter of ensuring, from the outset, that we would be
taken seriously, yet unstuffy enough to enjoy what had brought us all
together in the first place.

We decided that our robes would be worn only by those who had
been admitted to the fellowship (FBS) and that the guiding principle
(apart from designing something 'dignified and beautiful') should be
to have something with some kind of association with Dean Burgon
himself. Nicholas Groves alerted us to the fact that Burgon had been
a Fellow of Oriel College, Oxford, whose colours are dark blue and
silver and we discussed how best to incorporate these colours into
the robes along with the crimson of the Oxford MA hood (Burgon's
name was originally associated with a revised shape of the BA hood,
but is now also universally used for the Oxford MA).

'B' for Burgon

In the meantime, Dr Birch, although not yet President, was taking
an interest in our discussions about dress for the Society. He also

74 A quotation from Charles Franklyn's Academical Dress ...
75 See the Council minutes for 14 July 2001.

wanted to include a nod, in the proposed robes, to Burgon's Oxford connections by way of a 'B' for Burgon cut-out at the end of the glove sleeves and a crimson cord and button on the yoke of the FBS gown. He wrote to me on this subject in October 2000 and it was read out at the first meeting of the Burgon Society Council, at Senate House, University of London, on 21 October, 2000.

> Dear Philip,
>
> Further to our telephone conversation this morning, when you were kind enough to tell me of some of the exciting news for the Burgon Society. I summarised our conversation all-be-it on rather scholarly notepad rather than official paper for which I apologise.
>
> My suggestion for a fellows' gown would be the Oxford or Cambridge M.A., in each case with strings, but with facings, possibly 4 inches of Oxford MA hood lining, plus, of course, a cord and button on the yoke of the same.
>
> To me, the suggestion of a hood does not seem entirely convincing since it denotes an academic qualification, which presumably the fellowship and Membership will not be. Certainly, a hood has disadvantages, particularly when dining. One wearer got his hood full of petit-pois on one occasion! Since I now wear the Oxford D.Mus gown (tho' not as an Oxford graduate I hasten to add) I think, since the hood is never worn with an Oxford Doctors' Full dress gown, that this looks more distinguished than the comparable Mus.D/DMus Full Dress of Cambridge, Durham and Dublin with which the hood is worn. A gown, I think, looks v. distinguished on its own, and quite in keeping with such a society; the adoption of a hood might well look as if we were trying to be something that we are not and could damage the credibility and dignity of the Society which must be of significant importance in matters academic.
>
> Perhaps the Chairman might have an official robe of a black gown of the shape of the Oxford Doctors but with sleeves and facings of the Oxford MA hood lining. As a personalisation of the gown, why not have the ends of the glove sleeves in a B(urgon)? Just an idea.

On 20 November 2000, I wrote an email to the members of Council, part of which said:

> May we have a full response to the crimson cord and button question? My vote is still no but I could live with it if it is the desire of the majority.

The FBS hood

Notwithstanding Dr Birch's letter, there was little chance that a group of academic dress enthusiasts forming a new society were not going to design a hood for themselves and there were several excellent and attractive suggestions.[76]

There was much admiration for the dark blue silk hood, naturally, of the Burgon shape, lined and bound with (Oxford MA) shot crimson silk as Nicholas Groves reported in a follow-up email to Cyburcouncil after the inaugural meeting of the Society on 2 September 2001:

> We were greatly impressed by Phil Lowe's 'specimen' hood,[77] but the mind of the meeting was that the hood should be dark blue (Oxford/Oriel) lined with Oxford MA shot crimson— some debate as to whether the shell should be plain or brocade.

However, in attempting to source the fabrics from which to have a sample of the hood made, I discovered that the Oxford MA crimson silk, amongst all the main suppliers, was in a rather poor state; that the latest offerings of this silk from the silk weaving companies was rather thin and disappointing and that for some time only the flat crimson Oxford MA silk, or a rather strange bright orange silk were being used and supplied. What had happened to the shot silk consisting of a flame-coloured thread and a plum-coloured thread which was much loved, admired and recognized?

I alerted colleagues to the situation in an email on 13 November 2000:

> In the meantime I have been trying to get some sample hoods made up for us and have discovered a startling piece of

---

76 In fact, the Burgon Society has two fellowship hoods: the black s1 lined ruby silk hood described above and the winter hood, later referred to as the festal hood. The latter was authorised at a Council meeting on 4th July 2009. The Council minutes record it thus: '… modified Durham BCL shape, made of black cloth, lined with ruby shot silk and bound with 2" miniver. The fur on the presented hood was possum (grey); however, as it could be bleached, there will be no prescription as to the colour used ….' This all took place well beyond the timeframe of the present essay but it is hoped that a future volume of Transactions will include a full account of its introduction.

77 I think that this refers to a dark blue hood of the Burgon shape [s2] faced inside around the cowl with 3" shot crimson silk and faced around the outside of the cape with 2" of gold and blue, St Margaret brocade.

information. There is, at present, no proper blood shot crimson silk around.[78]

I have checked with all our suppliers and weavers and also checked with Robin Richardson at Wippells (who uses the same supplier as Shepherd & Woodward). New Oxon MA hoods these days are being made with the alternative flat crimson colour (which is authorised but dreary, I think). The so-called shot silk which we have been offered recently is awful and paper thin. This is a shameful state of affairs and part of a much wider story concerning silk weaving in this country. Please keep the substance of this e-mail confidential to ourselves. I am concerned about this and am currently having trials done. For the present however I am taking apart one of my 20 or so (correctly lined) Oxon MA hoods and will send the silk to be made up into some buttons for the backs of our MA style gowns. If I don't have any joy with the Oxon MA silk here, I will put it on my list to take to India in January. I suggest 30 line size buttons. Is everyone happy with this? If so, I will get them done and then dish them out. At least we can get the buttons right straight away! By the way, the regs say 'crimson cord and button'. I imagine this should be black cord and crimson button. A crimson cord would be different but a trifle naff?

Discussion about the FBS hood continued and the favourite was still the dark blue lined Oxford MA crimson silk. However, a feeling was growing in the Council that this hood was rather too close to that of the Oxford MA and might bring some negative criticism down upon us.

Ruby to the rescue

At Ede & Ravenscroft, I had come to admire another shot silk known as 'judges' ruby', which was used for the trimming on robes for se-

---

78 The background to this is quite interesting. In the 1980s silk-weaving companies had generally moved to new technology and had given up use of the old shuttle looms on which so many of the historic and well-known silks used in academic hoods were woven. This had consequences for robemakers and when, in 1996, I returned to working in the industry it had been rather dismaying to see what had happened to some of the silks, which clearly had departed in colour and quality from those I knew. This was particularly true for the shot silks which previously had been woven with a silk warp and rayon weft which gave a lustrous finish to the fabric. I mentioned earlier in this article the problem with the Wales Music/Royal College of Organists silk but because other robemakers made many more new Oxford robes than Ede & Ravenscroft I hadn't, at the time, appreciated the decline in the Oxford MA silk.

The Burgon Society.

Fellows' Hood (FBS)

© EDE AND RAVENSCROFT LTD. 2008

Figure 12. The FBS hood.

nior legal officers in Guernsey.[79] Moreover, in 1997, when I had been assisting with the revisions in the academic dress in the University of London and designing new robes, I had used the ruby silk for the new Specialist Doctor's robe and hood. I knew that there wasn't (at the time) a problem with the supply of this silk and, with the agreement of the other members of Council had a sample made up, using black corded artificial silk for the shell and the ruby silk for the lining and binding. This hood was one of those I had suggested at the inaugural meeting of the Society. Nevertheless, opinion amongst members was divided on whether the outer fabric should be of black or dark blue corded artificial silk.

In an email to the Council members on 9 December, I wrote:

> Some sample hoods came in yesterday. The black silk lined and bound ruby shot silk looks divine to my eyes. At some point, I can have one made-up in dark blue but do have a look at this one. I must see about a photo.

In the event, the sample was adopted for the fellowship hood at the next meeting of Council, on 13 January 2001. (See Fig. 12.) The minute reads:

> Academical Dress: Philip Goff showed the meeting an example of a possible fellows' hood. This was Burgon shape, black corded silk, lined and bound shot ruby silk. It was agreed to adopt this as the official hood. Proposed Michael Powell, seconded Nicholas Groves, agreed *nem. con.* Philip agreed to obtain a quote for producing the hood. Thanks were offered to Philip.

Nicholas Groves, very helpfully rationalized our decision on the FBS hood (ex post facto) by informing us that Dean Burgon had matriculated at Worcester College, Oxford, whose colours fitted our scheme:

> It is from Dean Burgon's two colleges that we take our colours—the corporate colours of blue, crimson, and white are from the Oriel colours of dark blue and silver, with the crimson of the Oxford MA hood lining added; the FBS hood, of black lined shot pink, comes from the Worcester colours of black and pink.

---

79 A combination of ivory and garnet-coloured threads giving a warm rose effect.

The Black Gown

Once we had established ourselves as founding fellows and members of Council, we wore gowns at our meetings and at Congregation. We particularly wanted Congregation to be somewhat solemn and re-strained as opposed to our annual garden party at which fellows, members and guests were encouraged to show off whatever robes they pleased. Since we all owned (and some of often wore) black gowns already there wasn't a lot of enthusiasm for Dr Birch's sug-gestion of a gown with sleeves that ended in a 'B' for Burgon, nor for the crimson cord and button. Rather we just wore whatever gowns to which we were entitled save the doctors amongst us who wore undress gowns rather than their full-dress robes. In practice, this meant a black gown with long hanging glove (or Tudor bag) sleeves. The regulation for this was written into the minutes of the Council meeting of 14 July 2001:

> The following amendment was agreed for the fellows' gown. The gown of the fellow's highest degree, or a black gown of the traditional Master's shape. Proposed: Peter Durant, sec-onded; Michael Powell. Agreed *nem. con.* (See Figs 10 and 11.)

We soon began to see that further prescription was going to be necessary, however. What if a new fellow was not already entitled to a traditional black master's gown? What if the gown they owned was of another colour?[80] Every time we tried to prescribe something loosely that would mean, in practice, a black gown at Congregation, we would come up against an exception. The matter was settled, el-egantly, by our webmaster, Peter Durant, in 2003.[81]

---

80 Such as the grey master's gown of York or the blue of East Anglia.

81 Peter Durant submitted a very useful paper in 2003, which, alas, falls outside the scope of this article but which was discussed and adopted at a meeting of Council on 6 September and recorded in the minutes thus:

Dress Regulations — The proposal posted on Cyburcoun-cil by the Webmaster was discussed and the following agreed:

...

Fellow's Gowns—To avoid over prescription, while main-taining some uniformity the follow wording was agreed: a black gown of the traditional master's shape; or any other suitable black gown to which they are entitled.

Figure 13. Fellows at the 2003 Congregation wearing the FBS gown and hood: (left to right) Giles Brightwell; Ian Johnson, Treasurer; Br Michael Powell; Susan North, archivist; Les Robarts, at the time not yet a fellow; Professor Bruce Christianson (prior to donning the Dean of Studies' robe).

Fig. 14. FBS dress at Congregation 2003 (left to right): Dr Alex Kerr, Peter Durant, Webmaster; Susan North, archivist; Professor Bruce Christianson.

Robes for Officers and Council Members

At the outset, we decided not to think too much about robes for the various officers of Council but simply to wear our fellowship gowns and hoods for formal events. This was because there was much to do in setting up the Society but also the question of cost, and as a young Society there were other calls upon our cash. The feeling of some of the members was that we might begin slowly with, perhaps, some robes for the President and Chairman and then add others later, particularly for the Registrar and Dean of Studies, and also for the Marshal.

At the inaugural meeting of the Society on 2 September 2000, and on Cyburcouncil, members considered Dr Birch's idea of robes in the Oxford doctor's shape, made from dark blue artificial silk, with front and sleeve facings of the Oxford MA crimson silk and with 2" silver lace on the outside edge for the President's robe; 1" for the Chairman and a similar dress robe for all other members of Council, but with no lace. Nicholas Groves records some of the discussion in an email later in the day:

> Ceremonial robes for Council were adumbrated: Oxon doctor's pattern, in dark blue with sleeves and facings of shot crimson, worn without the hood, but with Bishop Andrewes cap (as Cantab DD).

In the spring of the following year, on 24 April 2001, in an email to Council members I mentioned the robes again:

> Another possibility would be to leave the robe as Oxon drs shape with front and sleeve facings of Oxon shot crimson and with 1" silver oakleaf lace on the outside edge of the front facings. If not for President then how about for the Chairman's robe (hehe!) or with Judge's ruby? Certainly, one of the most beautiful and dignified ...
>
> On the Oxon crimson subject ... in Calcutta recently I had some trials done which are looking promising.

To assist our discussions, I had some drawings done of the proposed robes. One proposed robe for the President is in Fig. 15.

On 15 July, a day after the Council meeting, Nicholas Groves circulated a document about robes for the various Officers (see Fig. 16).

The Burgon Society.

President's Robe.

Figure 15. Proposed President's robe.

THE BURGON SOCIETY

Robes for the Officers

Ordinary Members of Council shall wear a robe of [d2] pattern, in dark blue. The facings and sleeves shall be covered with shot crimson (as used for the Oxford MA hood); there shall be a silver cord and button on the yoke. With this robe shall be worn a black cloth Bishop Andrewes cap.

The Chairman of Council shall wear a robe as for other Councillors, but it shall in addition be edged along the outer edge of each facing with 1" silver braid. His cap may have a crimson tuft.

The President shall wear a similar robe, but the facings shall be edged with 2" silver braid, and there shall be silver braid ½" wide around the sleeves where the crimson meets the blue, after the manner of the Durham PhD. His cap shall be of black velvet, with silver braid round the skull and a silver tuft.

Note 1: the material of the dark blue bodies of the robes is to be determined – either ribbed silk or cloth.

Note 2: No hoods are worn with these robes.

Note 3: the exact depth of the crimson facing on the sleeves is to be decided. It may be to within a few inches of the shoulder, as the Oxford style, or it may be a cuff of 9", as at Hertfordshire. The facings proper are to be 5" wide (ideally 3" at the shoulder, widening to 6" at the hem).

Note 4: The Patron shall, for the time being, wear the robes of his highest degree, or of the Society's Fellowship. A suggested robe is:
> in dark blue of [d4] pattern, the facings and collar covered with shot crimson; the facings and collar to be edged with 2" silver braid; the armholes to be bound with ½" silver braid; and a 2" bar of silver braid across the base of each sleeve. The cap shall be as for the President.

Nicholas Groves, MA, BMus, FBS, FSAScot
Director of Research
15 vij 01

Figure 16. Proposal for officers' robes.

On 18 July he wrote:

> I think the idea was that we would get the two posh ones first (Chair and Pres., not nec'y [sic] in that order). The rest of us will have to wear degree or FBS robes until such time as cash is available. Perhaps there is to be a pecking order as to who gets the next robe to be made – or perhaps we draw lots. (PG says the [d2] pattern is cheaper than the [d1] by the by. Don't know about [d4].)[82]

Professor Bruce Christianson posted a message at around the same time giving his preferred option for dress at Congregation: which, with hindsight, might have been the opportunity to adopt something really special: "I'd go for blue habit and scarf for council members, black gown underneath, hood on top, and the cap."

Later that day, on Cyburcouncil Dr John Horton responded to the message writing, "Well, I know we have been round the loop on this one at least once, but there is no arguing with the fact that a habit would be a lot cheaper than a robe ... ."

Br Michael Powell had floated the possibility of an epitoge to be worn upon the black gown, to which Dr Horton replied, "Another good idea. Where do epitoges fit on the financial scale?"

Next to the copy of this Cyburcouncil message, which I believe came from Peter Durant, he had written, 'not very English.' Another message was circulated on the following day, by Br Michael:

> I think I threw in the epitoge idea a long way back— though I don't know quite how that would be without a hood. I am just concerned that at this early stage we are talking about committing a considerable amount of money when we do not have much. Remember that the annual is not going to be cheap and I think that has to be our first priority. Yes we can plan for officer's robes but I think the actuality might be some way into the future.
>
> My short-term concern is that at our October AGM our guests should have some way of recognising us. I know that there will not be many FBS hoods around except for our own but that is not the point. I think it essential that every guest be greeted by at least one member of the Council and that he should be clearly recognisable as such even if it's by something as small as a ribbon or a rosette (like the Legion d'Honneur ones, not a dog show winner!) worn on the 'lapel' of the gown.

---

82 [d2] Oxford doctor's shape in the Groves classification system. [d3] is the Cambridge doctor's shape, and [d4] is the Cambridge LLD undress gown (without the lace).

Fig. 17. At the first Burgon Society Congregation, Saturday, 20 October 2001 (left to right): Dr Stephen James, Registrar; Nicholas Groves, Director of Research; Dr John Birch, President; the Revd Philip Goff, Chairman.

Nicholas Groves followed up his message by suggesting that officers' robes could be purchased when the funds were available but adding that in the meantime, for the autumn ceremony: "a ribbon or possibly high-class engraved plastic conference-style badges might be considered."

In the event, for the first Congregation in 2001, Council members wore black gowns and their FBS hoods and the President wore his Lambeth DMus robe and bonnet. (See Fig. 17.) Later, I found him a black velvet Canterbury cap with a gold bullion tassel that had once been worn by the Queen Mother when Chancellor of the University of London. For myself, as Chairman, I wore a vintage black velvet mortarboard with a silver bullion tassel and found blue mortarboards for the Registrar and Director of Research. These were temporary measures until we had decided the question of hats. As might be imagined for such a society, the discussions concerning our costumes continued!

At some point in our discussions, we decided to adopt the suggested colours for the officers' robes but to change the shape to that most often associated with the officers of the various UK universities.[83] I seem to remember that we thought Dr Birch's suggestion

83 [d4] Cambridge LLD undress gown (without the lace), also known

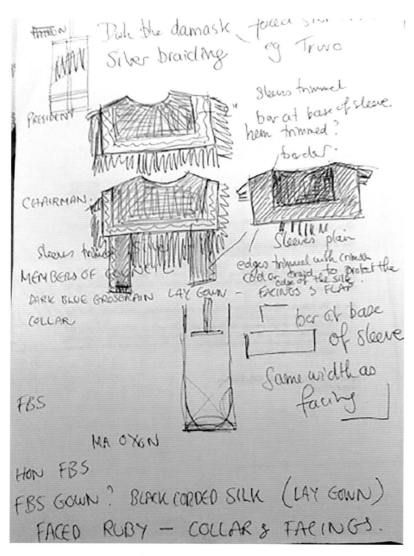

Figure 18. Philip Lowe's ideas for Officers' robes.

of the Oxford doctors' shape rather too suggestive of an academic degree and opted, in the end, for [d4] shape which Nicholas Groves had, suggested for the Patron.

At one of Council meetings, Philip Lowe who, amongst several other skills, is an independent robe and vestment maker, was busy doodling illustrations for the Officers' robes on the back of the minutes (see Fig. 18).

On 10 September, I wrote to the production manager at Ede & Ravenscroft Ltd, Marios Stylianou, as follows:

> Dear Mal,
>
> Is there a chance that, as a favour, you could do me three gowns in time for 20th October? (Ray tells me you are very busy but that things should get better in a few weeks' time).
>
> These robes are for a society of which I am the Chairman and several academics, who are known to us, are members.
>
> What I am looking for is as follows:
>
> 3 gowns in the QC style in dark blue CC artificial silk[84] all with facings of SW[85] rayon silk, Oxford MA shot crimson. The silk should continue around the flap collar or cover the flap collar – whichever is easier. All three gowns should be 56" long.
>
> 1 robe should have 2" of silver lace on the outside edge of the facings and around the collar and sleeve ends; and ½" silver lace around the 'T' cut at the armholes.
>
> 1 robe should be the same but with 1½" silver lace on the facings, around the collar and sleeve ends.
>
> 1 robe should have ½" silver lace on the facings and around the collar only.
>
> Would you please also supply another 6 FBS hoods: Black art silk of the larger (University of Westminster) Burgon shape lined and bound (as Oxford MA) with Judges' ruby silk.
>
> Perhaps we could speak about this on the 'phone?
>
> Phil

In the meantime, the Council decided that four officers' robes would be required, and I duly requested another one. The robes were for the President, Chairman, Registrar and the Director of Research (later, additionally, to become Dean of Studies). The robes were not ready in time for the first Congregation in October 2001 so I informed the production manager that they could be made up at as the QC shape.

84 'CC blue' refers to the colour of the robes worn by Councillors of Court of Common Council in the City of London.

85 Stephen Waters, a silk weaving company and supplier.

Fig 19. Director of Research (later Dean of Studies) Nicholas Groves and Chairman the Revd Philip Goff, wearing the new Officers' robes but before the Andrewes caps were adopted.

leisure but that it would be helpful to have a swatch of the fabrics for Council members to inspect.

At the Council meeting on 12 January 2002, I circulated samples of the dark blue artificial silk to be considered for the body of the officer's robes along with some of the Oxford MA shot crimson silk which I had had rewoven in India,[86] and some silver lace. The officers' robes were worn for the first time at the second Burgon Society Congregation on 19 October 2002, and in my report to the Council at the AGM (see Figs 19 and 20) earlier in the day, I said:

> Officers' robes for the President, Chairman, Registrar and Dean of Studies have been made for us courtesy of Ede and Ravenscroft. Robes for other members of Council can be made as and when possible. Designs for Bishop Andrewes' caps for all members of Council are still being made up as samples and alternatives are being used in the meantime.

The Marshal's Robes

Dr John Horton has been Marshal of the Burgon Society from the first Congregation in 2001 and oversees the ceremonial at formal events. The Marshal's robe, already venerable when I found it, was very well made by Ede & Ravenscroft, and probably dates from the 1940s or 50s (see Fig. 21). It is made of black corded silk of the [d4]

---

86 I was fortunate to have friends who ran a charity in Calcutta which they funded by employing an entire village in silk-weaving. Like many things, the shuttle looms hadn't died but had simply gone East! They were able to recreate the shot crimson Oxford MA taffeta and I encouraged Ede & Ravenscroft to buy it. I also made it available to other robemakers.

Fig 20. The Officers' robes at Congregation 2003: Professor Bruce Christianson, Dean of Studies; Dr James Thomson (Patron but here standing in for the President); Dr Alex Kerr (in the black gown and FBS hood); the Revd Philip Goff, Chairman; Dr Stephen James, Registrar.

Figure 21 (right). Marshal of the Burgon Society: Dr John Horton FBS.

pattern with 2¼" black velvet facings which continue round the neck to form a flap collar. It has wings at the shoulders and straight panel sleeves. It is decorated with Oxford gimp lace around the flap collar and at the armholes; and gimp pentagons at the bottom of the sleeves, either side at the bottom of the gown and centre back. The gown is worn with long academic bands. To begin with the Marshal wore his Cambridge PhD velvet bonnet with this gown but now wears a black Bishop Andrewes' cap with a crimson tuft (as a former member of the Burgon Council).

The Past and Future

In just over a year, a group of people, who had found an early internet group site on which to share information about their hobby, had met and formed themselves into a formal group for the study and enjoyment of academical dress. Far from being laughed at, the Burgon Society is a respected learned body with charitable status and is known internationally and throughout the worlds of academe, the robemaking industry and costume study. It continues to add to its membership those fascinated by the subject as well as those engaged in serious research for its fellowship. Led today by a new and younger generation, it continues to thrive and to make itself known through its excellent website and publications, including the journal. Its archive has grown into an important collection of dress, now safely stored, supervised and curated by a dedicated team, and its bibliography is unique in its catalogue of published textual and pictorial works.

What John William Burgon would make of the Society named after him,[87] were he alive today, is anyone's guess, and there is still some work to be done before anyone can say with confidence that he is responsible for the shape of an academic hood associated with his name. What we do know is that he was opposed to change and from an early age (his father was a keeper of antiquities) inclined towards the past albeit through the lens of literal Biblical rather than geological time. His biographer wrote:

> Whatever he had to do with habitually, whether a place, a person, a family, or an institution, he clothed it with such reverent affection, that it became sacred in his sight. To depreciate it, to alter it, to see any faults in it needing amendment, was sacrilege to be withstood with all his might.[88]
>
> "... How attired shall a man go forth to minister? A soiled curt surplice, stained with iron-mould, and unfurnished with hood or stole, crumpled bands, tied askew, and muddy boots, form an unseemly accompaniment (to say the least) for one who is to conduct the services of GOD'S House, however humble it may be. But is a man therefore driven into curious millinery, and the foppish extravagances of unpopular aestheticism? Need he appear in a surplice of peculiar cut, a stole embroidered with red, green, or yellow crosses, a hood so displayed that the crimson lining shall make him look positively smart, or wearing some unauthorized, or at least questionable vestment?"[89]

As for the choice of the ruby silk for the Society's fellowship hood, which just happened to be available—chosen and justified by

87 Not to be confused with the Dean Burgon Society which concerns itself with the defence of traditional biblical texts.

88 Edward Meyrick Goulburn, John William Burgon, Late Dean of Chichester: A Biography, 2 vols (London: John Murray, 1892), vol. II, p. 354.

89 Meyrick quoting Burgon, vol. II, pp. 10–11.

Fig. 22. Advertisement placed in the Church Times.

association with Burgon's own Worcester College—there is one curious reference worth recording that by coincidence or Providence brings the colour to mind.

In 1845, at the end of his undergraduate days at Oxford, Burgon wrote a poem called 'Petra' about the eponymous city, now in Jordan. The poem won Sir Roger Newdigate's Prize.[90] Part of it reads:

> It seems no work of Man's creative hand,
> By labour wrought as wavering fancy planned;
> But from the rock as if by magic grown,
> Eternal, silent, beautiful, alone!
> Not virgin-white like that old Doric shrine,
> Where erst Athena held her rites divine;
> Not saintly-grey, like many a minster fane,
> That crowns the hill and consecrates the plain;
> But rose-red as if the blush of dawn,
> That first beheld them were not yet withdrawn;
> The hues of youth upon a brow of woe,
> Which Man deemed old two thousand years ago,
> Match me such marvel save in Eastern clime,
> A rose-red city half as old as time.

There seems to me to be no reason why the Burgon Society should not continue to thrive far into the future, with ever new waves of academic dress enthusiasts to continue its original aims: to enjoy a fascinating hobby; to keep such dress and the traditions associated with it alive in an age in which, largely, it has become relegated to fewer events, and to pursue serious research in this branch of the history of dress, bedecked as it goes, in the Society's distinctive hood, 'rose-red as if the blush of dawn', if not yet 'half as old as time'.

---

90 '... awarded to students of the University of Oxford for the Best Composition in English verse by an undergraduate who has been admitted to Oxford within the previous four years ... The winning poem is announced at Encaenia.' (Wikipedia.) Burgon did not, in fact, visit Petra until Easter 1862, seventeen years after composing his poem.

Acknowledgments

It has been an agreeable task to write and collate this account of the founding of the Burgon Society in the knowledge that every one of the eleven founders, together with those others who were closely associated with us in its early years, have contributed to the piecing together of the story. This has afforded us much pleasure as we have looked back over our records and have shared (and sometimes corrected) our memories, reliving the fun of those exciting days at the beginning of a new millennium. After twenty years, perceptions of what took place can become distorted, so it has been most useful to have the written records of our meetings, but relying on these alone would have left several gaps in the account. It is, therefore, most fortuitous that we have benefited from the foresight of Dr Nicholas Jackson, FBS, who preserved a record of the email messages of Br Michael Powell's academic dress eGroup through which we can trace the developing conversation which led to our meetings and, subsequently, the Burgon Society.

I should like to thank my fellow founders for many useful suggestions, additions and corrections to the early text of this monograph and Professor Bruce Christianson, FBS, in particular, for reading through and helping to improve the later versions

As always, I thank the editor, Professor Stephen Wolgast, FBS, for his encouragement, courtesy, patience and skill in preparing this article for publication.

Constitution of the Burgon Society as agreed at the foundation meeting, 21 October 2000

Constitution of the Burgon Society

NOTE: in the following regulations, the pronoun 'he' shall, unless the context dictates to the contrary, be read as including 'she'.

1. The name of the Society shall be the BURGON SOCIETY, named after Dean Burgon, the only eponym of an academical hood—*vidz* the burgon shape.

2. The Society shall concern itself with the study of academical dress in all its aspects—design, practice, history.

3. The Society shall comprise:

(a) FELLOWS, who shall have demonstrated a significant contribution to one of the said aspects;

(b) MEMBERS, who shall be in sympathy with the aims of the Society, and who shall be encouraged to undertake research which can be presented for fellowship (see 7., *infra*).

All applications shall be approved by Council. Whilst Membership shall be the normative entry level, applicants may, if they have demonstrated due cause, be elected direct into fellowship.

4. The Society may confer on persons who have made an outstanding contribution to any area of the subject, the distinction of HONORARY FELLOW. They shall be entitled to vote for the President (see 11, *infra.*), but not to vote at meetings.

5. Fellows shall pay an annual subscription as Council determines from time to time, for which they shall be entitled to receive all publications and other mailings of the Society, and to vote at meetings; Members shall pay a subscription as Council determines from time to time, for which they shall be entitled to receive such mailings as Council deems fit, and to attend meetings, but not to vote.

6. Fellows may use the post-nominal designation FBS and wear the Society's hood; Members may do neither of these things.

7. Members may proceed to fellowship either on the presentation of a paper of approximately one hour's duration (or a series of shorter papers which forms the equivalent) at a meeting of the Society specially called for that purpose; or on the publication in the Society's Annual or another approved publication of an article of 5,000 words (or a series of shorter articles which forms the equivalent) on one of the aspects specified in 2 above, or by demonstrating in some other way a significant academic contribution. In each case, the application shall be discussed and voted on by the Council.

8. There shall be a Council of Management, elected by the fellowship, which shall comprise ELEVEN senior fellows. The following officers shall be elected: Chair of Council; Treasurer; Registrar; Membership Secretary; Director of Research; Editor; Communications Officer; and four ordinary Members of Council. The Archivist and Webmaster shall sit on Council ex officio. There may be other posts created as need dictates—e.g. an Excursions Secretary—which shall be filled by co-option.

9. In the case of a Member being elected to an Office, he shall be created a fellow *de jure*; in the case of a non-member of the Society being elected to an Office, he shall be offered a fellowship either *honoris causa* or *de jure* as the Council shall see fit.

10. The duties of the several Officers shall be as follows:

(a) Chair of Council: shall chair all Council Meetings and other ordinary meetings of the Society; he shall present newly-qualified fellows to the President for admission;

(b) Treasurer: shall have oversight of the Society's finances. He shall set up and maintain a bank account, and shall present each year properly audited accounts to the Annual Meeting;

(c) Registrar: shall act as secretary to meetings of Council and at ordinary meetings of the Society; he shall keep and maintain the Roll of Members, including details of work submitted and accepted for fellowship;

(d) Membership Secretary: shall receive and process applications for membership; shall maintain a membership list, and, with the Treasurer, see that all subscriptions are paid up to date;

(e) Director of Research: shall keep records of ongoing research undertaken by Members and fellows; shall oversee the production and presentation of work in submission for fellowship;

(f) Editor: shall edit the Annual, and other occasional publications of the Society;

(g) Communications Officer: shall liaise with universities, museums and other collections and other societies concerned with the history of dress; shall act as Press Officer; shall send complaints of inaccurate usage to the film or television company concerned;

(h) Webmaster: shall maintain the website;

(i) Archivist: shall maintain the archive.

11. There shall also be a PRESIDENT, elected by the fellows and Honorary fellows. He shall be elected for a period of FIVE years and may be elected for subsequent terms. If not already a fellow, he shall be created a fellow *jure Dignitatis.*

12. One or more PATRONS may be elected by the fellows and Honorary fellows if so desired.

13. Meetings shall be held from time to time, at which papers shall be presented for discussion. The public may be admitted. There

shall be a General Meeting every year. Other meetings, in the form of outings, may be held as deemed desirable. Papers shall be published in an Annual.

14. The Society may affiliate itself to other organizations which promote the study of costume. This shall be subject to a decision of the Council.

15. A website shall be set up and maintained by the Webmaster.

16. An archive (organized in two parts—the Library and the Wardrobe) shall be maintained by the Archivist, with especial reference to the past practices of institutions, preserving the details of superseded or otherwise obsolete robes. This archive shall take the form of paper documents (including photographs and other pictorial representations) and actual items of dress. It shall be available for consultation by interested parties in such ways as the Society determines.

17. It shall be proper for the Society to act in an advisory capacity to film and television producers, or others who wish to ensure correctness in dress; also to those who wish to design robes themselves. It may also undertake commissions to design robes. NB: any fellow is at liberty to act in a private advisory capacity but must make it plain that he does not act in this case for the Society.

18. In the event of the Society being wound up, such monies as remain over shall be given to an organization specified by Council.

19. This Constitution, having been once ratified at a General Meeting of the Society, may only be altered by a further General Meeting called for that purpose.

20. Any Member or fellow found guilty of conduct which, in the view of Council, causes the Society to be brought into disrepute, shall be subject to such penalty as Council shall deem fit, up to and including removal from the Roll of Members. In all such cases, the Member or fellow in question shall have the right of presenting a defence to Council.

21. Fellows may wear the academical robes of the Society.

22. Officers shall wear the ceremonial robes of the Society on occasions determined by Council.

AGREED UPON this 21st day of October 2000.

About the author

After reading Theology at King's College, University of London, Philip Goff spent 40 years working in London and its suburbs, as Assistant Curate at St Martin's Church Ruislip; Chaplain and Head of Religious Studies, Aldenham School, Elstree; Vicar of St Michael's Church, Wembley; Assistant Priest at Our Lady of Grace Church, Chiswick; Academic Consultant to Ede and Ravenscroft Ltd; Senior Practice Counsellor at Clapham Family Practice; Psychotherapist in private practice; Chaplain to the Bishop of Edmonton; Vicar of St Augustine's Church, Highgate and Area Dean of West Haringey.

In 2015 he retired and divides his time between the UK and Thailand, returning each year to enjoy the English springtime and to take care of his bees. He is a Fellow of the Society of Antiquaries and a founder of the Burgon Society.